COURSE COMPANION

# Health and Social Care

DIPLOMA LEVEL **2**

## Val Michie

Contributing author:
**Eleanor Langridge**

Nelson Thornes

Published in 2012 by:
Nelson Thornes Ltd
Delta Place
27 Bath Road
CHELTENHAM
GL53 7TH
United Kingdom

12 13 14 15 16 / 10 9 8 7 6 5 4 3 2 1

A catalogue record for this book is available from the British Library

ISBN 978 1 4085 1535 8

Cover photograph: iStock/© Brian Jackson
Illustrations by Angela Lumley and Peters and Zabransky UK Ltd
Page make-up by Fakenham Prepress Solutions, Norfolk
Printed and bound in Spain by GraphyCems

Photo acknowledgements
Corbis: © Beau Lark p119; fotolia: © iceteastock p66; iStock: © Chris
Schmidt p1; © Nicole S.Young pp24, 47; © Maxine Lawson p80; ©
sturti p102; © NuStock p147; © Alistair Forrester Shankie p168; © Paula
Connelly p176; © Iain Sarjeant p192; SCIENCE PHOTO LIBRARY: AJ
PHOTO p210.

# Contents

# Introduction

Welcome to the Health and Social Care Level 2 Diploma Course Companion. It is a companion to support you throughout your course and record your progress.

This workbook-style book is designed to be used alongside **any** student book you are using. It is packed full of activities for you to complete in order to check your knowledge and reinforce the essential skills you need for this qualification.

Features of the Course Companion are:

**Unit opener** – this page contains a brief introduction to each unit along with the learning objectives you need to achieve.

**Activities** – a wide variety of learning activities are provided for you to complete in your Companion. Each activity is linked to one of the Personal, Learning and Thinking Skills to help you practise these fundamental skills:

 – Reflective Learner

 – Creative Thinker

 – Teamworker

 – Self Manager

 – Independent Enquirer

 – Effective Participator

You will also notice additional icons that appear on different activities, these link to the following core skills and also to employment rights and responsibilities in the workplace:

 – Literacy

 – Numeracy

 – ICT

 – Employment, Rights and Responsibilities

**Case studies** – a range of real life examples of different scenarios to provide context to the topics covered. Case studies are also linked to one of the Personal, Learning and Thinking Skills and the core skills or employment rights and responsibilities in the workplace (where appropriate).

**Key terms** – during your course you'll come across new words or new terms that you may not have heard before, so definitions for these have been provided.

**Assessor tip** – tips and advice are provided by an experienced assessor to help you demonstrate competency and build your portfolio.

**Your questions answered** – your expert author, Val Michie, answers some burning questions you may have as you work through the units.

**Are you ready for assessment?** – at the end of each unit you will find a checklist of the skills and knowledge covered in the unit. If you're confident you have covered these, then you're ready for assessment!

Good luck!

# UNIT SHC 21

## Introduction to communication in health and social care settings

**The ability to communicate well is very important, particularly in health and social care settings.**

Good communication with the people you care for and support is about getting to know them as individuals, finding out their needs and preferences for the way they communicate, making sure you understand each other and remaining professional and trustworthy at all times. Poor communication means that mistakes are made and people's needs are not met appropriately. To do your job well, you need to develop and use good, effective communication skills.

### You will need to be able to:

* understand the importance of communication at work
* meet communication and language needs, wishes and preferences
* reduce barriers to communication
* apply principles and practices relating to confidentiality at work.

# The importance of communication at work

## Reasons why people communicate

Effective communication ensures that people's needs are met appropriately.

There are three main reasons why people communicate.

* ✿ To let others know how they feel and what they want, for example that they need to go to the toilet or are thirsty and want a drink of water.
* ✿ To find things out and get answers to their questions, for example to find out hospital visiting times and whether there is a vegetarian option on the menu.
* ✿ To pass on information and give directions, for example to describe a patient's condition to a doctor and to tell someone how to give emergency first aid.

  **ACTIVITY**

Think about three people you support (patients, service users), a colleague and a manager. For each of these people, give an example of why you communicate with them.

✿ Patient/service user 1:

✿ Patient/service user 2:

✿ Patient/service user 3:

✿ A colleague:

✿ A manager:

ACTIVITY

Communication is a two-way process where messages are sent and received between individuals to ensure that each makes sense of what the other wishes to convey. Messages may include verbal and non-verbal communication (see page 7). The diagram below explains the communication cycle. Complete the cycle by adding the missing words from the list provided.

message    sees    repeats    sense    hears

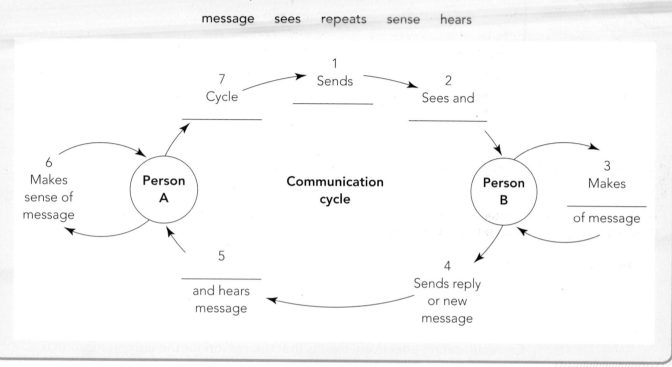

7
Cycle
_____

1
Sends
_____

2
Sees and
_____

6
Makes
sense of
message

Person
A

Communication
cycle

Person
B

3
Makes
_____
of message

5
_____
and hears
message

4
Sends reply
or new
message

## Mary

 CASE STUDY

Mary, who has dementia, has fallen and broken her hip. She has been accompanied to hospital by a care worker from the residential care home where she lives.

1. State three things that the people involved in Mary's care need to share with hospital staff to make sure she receives the best possible support.

   (Clue – the people involved in Mary's care include Mary herself, her friends and relatives, the residential care home staff and the hospital staff.)

✿

✿

✿

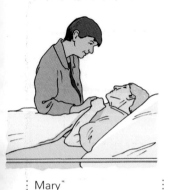

Mary

2. What could happen if the people involved in Mary's care don't communicate effectively with each other and with her?

## Effective communication in your work

Health and social care is provided by a team of people. The role of the team is to work together to provide care that is appropriate and meets people's needs. You need to be able to communicate effectively with everyone in your team, which includes the people you support, their families and friends, as well as:

* your colleagues
* senior staff and managers
* other workers, such as administrative and domestic staff, tradespeople and visiting health and social care professionals.

Communicating effectively means that the reason for the communication is successfully achieved. For example, during a health emergency you ask a colleague to call for help, they understand your request, call for help, help arrives and the situation is resolved. If your communication had been ineffective time may have been lost in further explanation and the outcome for the injured individual may have been quite different.

If you don't share information with everyone in your team, if you fail to respond to how they feel and what they want and need, and don't ask them questions or follow their directions, then the people you support will not be cared for appropriately and their needs won't be met.

## Reasons for communicating and how effective communication affects my work activity

  **ACTIVITY**

Complete the boxes by adding the following:

* A reason why you need to communicate with this person.
* What might happen if you didn't communicate effectively with them.

Also try to add an example of a colleague who is not a member of the care team and another professional.

| Service users | Care staff colleagues |
|---|---|
| | |

| Family members | Other colleagues e.g. _____ |
|---|---|
| | |

| Manager | Other professionals e.g. _____ |
|---|---|
| | |

## Your questions answered...

I'm really worried because I forgot to tell Mr Jones that his daughter had rung to say she couldn't visit him at the care home this afternoon. Mr Jones looks forward to seeing her, he depends on her visits and he's devastated that she hasn't turned up. What can I do? I feel dreadful.

We're all human and we all make mistakes. Fortunately, this isn't a life or death mistake to have made, but it is one from which you can learn. The best thing to do would be to tell Mr Jones that you're very sorry, you meant to tell him about the phone call but it completely slipped your mind. No excuses. Tell the truth. However, don't forget to pass on information again.

# The importance of observing people's reactions when communicating with them

The way someone reacts to what you're telling them can mean that:

- they haven't understood you or you haven't understood them
- they haven't heard you
- they're not interested in what you're telling them, have other things on their mind or are busy and don't have time for you at the moment

5

✿ they're pleased or upset by what you have told them

✿ they enjoy your company or there's something about you they don't quite like.

Unless you make a point of checking someone's reactions when you ask them for information, answer their questions or follow their instructions, you won't know whether your communication has been effective or not. Ineffective communication leads to misunderstandings, mistakes and care that is inappropriate.

## ACTIVITY

**What do these faces tell you about how people feel?**

_____          _____

_____          _____

_____          _____

_____          _____

_____

## ACTIVITY

Much of the communication between you, as a worker, and the individuals you support will be based on building and maintaining a working relationship with those people. Listening and using empathy will be important aspects of this process. Think about the people you support and their relatives. Reflect on how you communicate with them and how this may be different to the way in which you communicate with colleagues.

List at least four ways in which you can communicate more effectively with service users and relatives.

✿

✿

✿

✿

# Communication and language needs, wishes and preferences

## Finding out about communication and language needs, wishes and preferences

We communicate through speech (verbal communication), through body language (non-verbal communication) and with the use of communication aids and technology.

## ACTIVITY

Complete the following sentences to show your knowledge of how to communicate effectively.

1. To communicate effectively using verbal communication, I must:

   ✿

   ✿

   ✿

2. To communicate effectively using non-verbal communication, I must:

   ✿

   ✿

   ✿

3. Examples of aids and technology that can be used to help effective communication include:

   ✿

   ✿

   ✿

## key terms

**Vocabulary:** the words we use.
**Translator:** someone who converts one language into another.
**Interpreter:** someone who explains the meaning of words.
**Sensory impairment:** damage to, or weakness in, one of the senses, for example seeing or hearing.
**Advocate:** someone who speaks on another person's behalf.
**Communication and technological aids:** these aids include symbols, pictures, photographs, writing, sign language, interpreters, translators and special computer programs.
**Cultural background:** the customs, behaviours, beliefs and values that you were brought up with.

We're all different and our differences show in the way we communicate. The way we communicate differs according to:

✿ our language and accent and the **vocabulary** we use. Having a conversation with someone who speaks a different language or has a strong accent can be difficult. You might need a **translator.** Jargon (technical vocabulary) is difficult to understand unless you use it yourself. You may need an **interpreter**.

✿ our ability to use and understand communication. Someone with learning difficulties, a **sensory impairment** or a physical disability may find it difficult to communicate. We say they have special needs. They may need an **advocate** or help in the form of **communication and technological aids**.

✿ our **cultural background**. Different cultures have different beliefs about what is respectful when using body language, for example touch and eye contact.

✿ our age. For example, an older person may prefer you use their full name rather than just their first name, as they may feel this is more respectful.

To care for people appropriately, you need to find out how to communicate with them in a way that meets their individual needs, wishes and preferences. You can do this by:

✿ asking them
✿ asking relatives, friends or other professionals involved in their care and support
✿ reading reports, care plans and other records
✿ being aware of their culture, nationality or ethnicity
✿ observing their responses.

## ACTIVITY

The Accident and Emergency Department (A & E) at the hospital where you work serves a very diverse community, with patients of every age, ability and background.

How would you help someone attending A & E to tell you what's wrong with them if they:
1. don't speak the same language as you?

2. are older?

3. are deaf?

4. are blind?

Different ways of communicating

5. are unable to speak clearly because they've had a stroke?

6. are unable to understand because they have a learning difficulty?

7. have a different religious or cultural background from you?

## Show you can use communication methods that meet people's language needs, wishes and preferences

  **ACTIVITY**

Keep a diary for a week to show when you have used the following communication methods appropriately.

❀ Verbal communication, such as using words that are easily understood, using the correct tone of voice, speaking clearly and at an appropriate speed (not too fast), and speaking at a volume that people can hear (not shouting).

- Non-verbal communication, such as listening attentively, maintaining eye contact to show interest, using facial expressions and body movements to show respect and understanding, not slouching and not touching, unless you have permission.
- Communication and technological aids, including symbols, pictures, photographs, writing, sign language, interpreters, translators and special computer programs.

> **MONDAY**
>
> Today I had to tell Mrs Evans that her medication is changing. I had to speak slowly and clearly because she's a bit deaf. I had to explain in simple language why her meds are changing because the doctor used a lot of jargon that she didn't understand. I watched her and asked her questions to check that she understood me. She did understand but said she's fed up with all these changes. I said I'm sure she is and squeezed her hand. She likes that; it puts her mind at rest.

Keeping a diary

## How and when you should seek advice about communication

There are a number of sources of help and advice you can use if you're worried that communication problems might affect the care and support you give. Some of them, for example patients and service users, their relatives and friends, your colleagues and manager, are easy to find for help and advice. Others, such as translators and interpreters, speech and language therapists and advocates, may work in a hospital, for the local authority or for a charitable or private sector organisation.

## ACTIVITY

The following people and services can give help and advice regarding communication problem. When would you use them? Draw a line to match them up.

| People and services in health and social care | When would you use them? |
| --- | --- |
| The people you support. | Any time I have a problem, as they might have more experience than me. |
| Relatives and friends of the people you support. | For people who have a problem speaking and making themselves understood. |
| Your colleagues. | For problems experienced by their relative or friend, as they know them best and know how to help. |
| Your manager. | To explain the meaning of words. |
| Translation services. | Any time there is a problem, as they are the experts and know what help they need. |
| Interpreting services. | For people who have difficulties speaking for themselves, such as people with learning difficulties. |
| Speech and language therapists (SALTS). | Any time I have a problem, but especially when colleagues can't help. |
| Advocacy services. | To help where there are language differences. |

# Reducing barriers to communication

## What are the barriers to communication?

If communication is to be effective, people must be able to express themselves clearly and understand each other. Barriers prevent effective communication taking place. Communication barriers in health and social care settings mean that people are not cared for appropriately and their needs are not met. Barriers may result from any of the following.

- ✿ Environmental factors, for example noise.
- ✿ The individual's stage of development.
- ✿ Ill health, distress or emotional difficulties.
- ✿ Sensory impairment or disability.
- ✿ Language or cultural difficulties.
- ✿ Unfamiliar language, for example slang.

## Show you can reduce barriers to communication in different ways

Barriers to communication can be reduced through simple actions such as turning off the television or radio or sitting in a quiet, well lit  place when talking to someone; using familiar language; speaking clearly and slowly; making sure the individual is physically comfortable or through adopting open and non-threatening body language. Some barriers, such as language differences, may require using an interpreter and can be more complex to arrange.

## ACTIVITY

Talk to five people you support and ask them what problems they experience when trying to communicate. Make a note of what they tell you below and identify at least two ways in which each barrier could be reduced.

| Barrier to communication | Two ways to reduce this barrier |
|---|---|
|  |  |
|  |  |
|  |  |
|  |  |
|  |  |

## Community House

### CASE STUDY

Community House is a community social care setting. It provides English language classes for asylum seekers who originate from non-English-speaking countries. It runs self-help groups for people who have had a stroke, have dementia and have mental health problems.

The staff at Community House are rushed off their feet. They have very little time to sit with the service users and build relationships.

Suggest five barriers to communication that people might experience at Community House and say how you would help to reduce them.

✿

✿

✿

✿

✿

**Assessor tip**

Remember, you will be able to show your assessor how you communicate, and reduce barriers to communication, each time they observe you undertaking a work activity. You will also need to think about potential barriers to your communication with them when preparing for workplace assessment.

## Checking that communication has been understood

How do you know that people fully understand what you tell them? Or that you have properly understood what someone has told you? Misunderstandings can lead to mistakes and, in a health and social care setting, mistakes lead to care that is inappropriate and that doesn't meet people's needs. So, you must always check that any communication you take part in is properly understood.

## ACTIVITY

Complete the gaps in the following sentences using the words below to show you know how to make sure a communication is fully understood.

impatient    body language    closed    paraphrasing    gestures
open questions    repeating    interrupt    facial expressions

✿ Ask _____ _____ to find out if the person fully understands what you've said.

✿ _____ questions which require no more than a 'Yes' or 'No' answer, do not give people an opportunity to show their understanding or express their feelings about what you've told them. Give them time to think about what you've said. Don't _____ and don't put words into their mouths!

✿ Check people's _____ _____ as you communicate with them. Confused or quizzical _____ _____ and _____, such as shoulder shrugs, will tell you that they don't understand. On the other hand, head nods, thumbs up and murmurings, such as 'mmm', confirm understanding.

✿ If the person becomes bored or _____, for example they look away or tap their feet, you've lost their attention, which means they won't understand you. You'll have to try again, in a different way!

✿ Check your understanding by _____ back to the person, in your own words, what you think you've been told. This is called _____. It also gives the person an opportunity to check that you've understood correctly!

## Sources of information and support and services to enable more effective communication

You looked earlier at sources of information and support and services to help with communication. The next activity gives you an opportunity to confirm your knowledge.

 **ACTIVITY**

Complete the crossword with people who are a source of information to enable effective communication. The first and last letters of each answer have been left in as extra clues to help you.

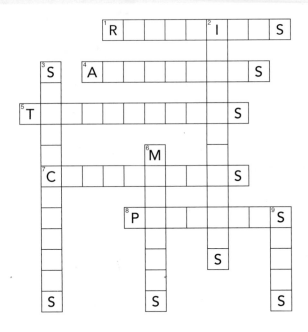

**Across**

1. Family members
4. People who speak on behalf of others
5. People who convert one language into another
7. People you work with
8. People cared for in a health care setting

**Down**

2. People who explain the meaning of words
3. People supported in a social care setting (two words)
6. Your superiors at work
9. Acronym for people who help others with their speech and language

# Applying principles and practices relating to confidentiality at work

## What do we mean by 'confidentiality'?

Confidentiality is to do with being discreet and keeping things private. We all have a right to have information about us kept confidential. Promoting the right to confidentiality of the people you support develops their trust in you, which, in turn, encourages them to confide what you need to know so you can meet their needs appropriately.

## ACTIVITY

1. What sort of information about you would you want to keep private?

..................................................................................................................................................

..................................................................................................................................................

..................................................................................................................................................

..................................................................................................................................................

..................................................................................................................................................

2. Think about an occasion when someone told another person something about you that you wanted to keep private. How did you feel?

..................................................................................................................................................

..................................................................................................................................................

..................................................................................................................................................

..................................................................................................................................................

## ACTIVITY

Use an internet search engine to search for the eight rules of the **Data Protection Act 1998**. Complete the gaps in the following sentences using the words below.

> relevant   European Economic Area   accurate   reason   fairly   safe   rights
>
> no longer than necessary   lawfully   up-to-date   collected   secure   adequate

The eight rules of the Data Protection Act 1998 state that personal and sensitive data must be:

✿ processed _____ and _____. This means the

person should be told why you are collecting their information, what you are

going to do with it, and who you may share it with.

✿ only used for the _____ it was _____ . For

example, personal information on a patient administration system must only

be used for health care reasons, not for looking up friends' addresses or

birthdays.

### key term

**Data Protection Act 1998:** this Act protects our right to keep our personal and sensitive information (known as data) confidential.

- _____ and _____ for the reason it was collected. Only collect and keep information you need. Don't collect information just in case it might be useful in the future.

- _____ and _____-_____-_____. Be careful when recording information to make sure it is correct and check to make sure it is current.

- kept for _____ _____ _____ _____. Destroy information when it is no longer needed – don't keep it just in case it might be useful in the future.

- used according to the _____ of the person involved. For example, don't give information to someone else if the person hasn't given their permission.

- kept _____ and _____. This applies to confidential conversations as well as confidential information that is written down.

- kept within the _____ _____ _____. Information may not remain confidential when taken outside of the EEA.

## key term

**Agreed ways of working:** these tell you how you must carry out your work activities.

# Show you use confidentiality in your day-to-day communication in line with agreed ways of working

Your workplace should have a policy, **agreed ways of working** (policies and procedures) that describe how workers must comply with the Data Protection Act 1998. Other legislation (or laws) that will have influenced organisational policies and procedures include the following:

- The Mental Capacity Act 2005: this ensures procedures are in place to support individuals who lack the capacity to make a decision.
- The Freedom of Information Act 2000: this covers the right to ask a public organisation for information, which doesn't include personal details and which is not included in the Data Protection Act.
- The Computer Misuse Act 1990: secures computer programmes and confidential data through authorisation protocols and makes unauthorised access or alteration a criminal offence.

## ACTIVITY

1.  Ask to see your workplace's policy about maintaining confidentiality of information. Make notes below about what it tells you.

2.  Ask your manager which of your workplace procedures/agreed ways of working on confidentiality of information apply to you in your day-to-day communication. Make notes below about what s/he tells you.

3.  Keep a diary for a week to record how you have used these procedures/agreed ways of working in your day-to-day communication.

## ACTIVITY

Think about the potential consequences of a worker breaching (breaking) confidentiality for the following people.

1.  The individual whose confidentiality has been broken:

2.  The worker:

3.  The employer/organisation:

## Situations when confidential information might need to be passed on

Breaking confidentiality (disclosure) means passing on information about someone without their permission. In such a situation, information must only be disclosed to someone with a 'need to know' and, except in exceptional cases, the person involved must be told exactly what information about them has been passed on.

### ACTIVITY

Complete the table to show that you understand when it is acceptable to break confidentiality.

| Reason for disclosure | Example |
|---|---|
| When people behave in ways that put their own health and well-being at risk. | |
| When people behave in ways that put other people's health and well-being at risk. | |
| When people have an infectious disease that puts other people's health at risk. | |
| When someone is being abused. | |

### ACTIVITY

Think about the examples you have given in the previous activity and what might happen if the information was not disclosed for each of the following people.

1. The individual disclosing the information:

2. The worker:

3. The employer/organisation:

## How and when to seek advice about confidentiality

There will be occasions when you're asked for information that you are not sure you can give. There will also be occasions when someone tells you something but wants you to promise not to tell anybody. What can you do in such situations?

 **ACTIVITY**

How would you manage the following situations?

1. Someone phones saying they are from the bank and need Mr Pimley's internet banking details. Mr Pimley has cerebral palsy and can't answer the phone. You are his care assistant and help him with his online banking.

2. A woman you don't recognise comes to the reception desk at the hospice where you volunteer, asking the whereabouts of one of the patients. She says the patient is her mother and she has come to get the house key so she can do a spring clean.

3. It is the evening shift and a man in overalls rings the doorbell at the care home where you work. He tells you through the intercom that he is the electrician who has been called to fix the burglar alarm. You weren't expecting him.

4. Simon drops into the conversation that he is growing cannabis in his flat. You've been his social worker for a number of years and have a good relationship with him. He asks you not to mention the cannabis to anyone.

## Assessor tip

Remember to maintain confidentiality when gathering evidence for your diploma. Never include personal records in your portfolio and never use names or other identifying information when using real work examples to demonstrate your knowledge and understanding.

## ARE YOU READY FOR ASSESSMENT?

☑ **Do you know the following:**

☐ **1.** The reasons why people communicate?

☐ **2.** How to communicate effectively with people you work with?

☐ **3.** The reasons for observing an individual's reactions when communicating with them?

☐ **4.** Sources of information and support or services to enable more effective communication?

☐ **5.** The meaning of confidentiality?

☐ **6.** The circumstances when it is appropriate to pass confidential information on?

☑ **Can you do the following:**

☐ **1.** Find out an individual's communication needs, wishes and preferences?

☐ **2.** Use a range of communication methods to meet individual needs, wishes and preferences and ensure that communication has been understood?

☐ **3.** Show how and when to seek advice about communication?

☐ **4.** Demonstrate how to reduce barriers to communication in different ways?

☐ **5.** Maintain confidentiality of information through your daily work activities?

# UNIT SHC 22

## Introduction to personal development in health and social care settings

To make sure that you meet the needs of the people you care for and support, you need to develop your knowledge and understanding, learn new skills and stay up-to-date in your work practice. This is called personal development. Personal development ensures that you support people appropriately and to a high standard. It also increases your chances of promotion and helps you stay fulfilled in your job.

### You will need to be able to:
* understand what is required for competence in your work role
* reflect on your work activities
* agree a personal development plan
* develop your knowledge, skills and understanding.

# Competence in your work role

Competence is about how well you do your job. If you're competent, you carry out your **duties and responsibilities** with knowledge, understanding and skill. If you're incompetent, you're unskilled and ineffectual. There are many standards and regulations that help you to become competent. In addition, you can help yourself by making sure that your attitudes and beliefs don't obstruct the way you work.

If you are not sure what your duties and responsibilities are, or if you do not have a job specification, ask your manager at once.

Your role and responsibilities are also guided by the following.
* National Occupational Standards (NOS), for example diploma standards.
* Codes of Practice, for example the General Social Care Council (GSCC) Code of Practice for Social Care Workers.
* Regulations, for example Care Quality Commission (CQC) Essential Standards of Quality and Safety.

You can find the GSCC Code of Practice for Social Care Workers at www.gscc.org.uk and the CQC Essential Standards of Quality and Safety at www.cqc.org.uk/standards.

Although health care workers do not have a specific code of practice, the Royal College of Nursing (RCN) website contains a lot of information regarding the health care assistant role and accountability. It also contains information related to the delegation of tasks by health care professionals to them. See www.rcn.org.uk.

## key term

**Duties and responsibilities:** work activities a person is required to do according to their job specification.

## The duties and responsibilities of your job role

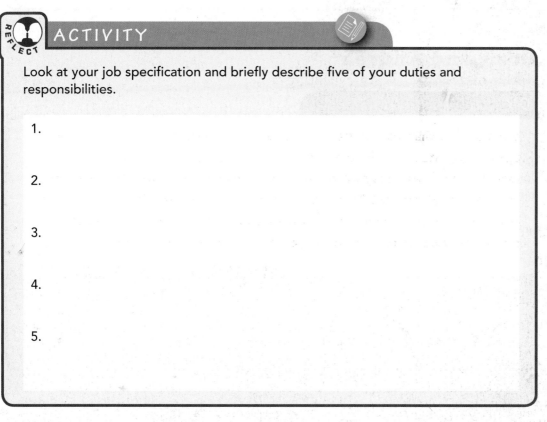

**ACTIVITY**

Look at your job specification and briefly describe five of your duties and responsibilities.

1.

2.

3.

4.

5.

For each duty and responsibility, think about what you are competent at and what you are not so good at.

| | What I do well | What I'm not so good at |
|---|---|---|
| 1. | | |
| 2. | | |
| 3. | | |
| 4. | | |
| 5. | | |

## Doris and Andrea

### CASE STUDY

Doris has multiple sclerosis and Andrea, her support worker, comes in twice a day to help her get up, have a bath, use the toilet, prepare meals, get ready for bed and so on. Andrea is often late, has little interest in cooking and what Doris likes to eat and drink, her personal hygiene leaves a lot to be desired, she is overweight and grumbles about having to 'haul' Doris around.

1. In what ways do you think Andrea is incompetent?

2. How might Andrea's incompetence affect the way she supports Doris?

3. If you were Doris, how do you think you might feel about Andrea?

## Standards that influence the way you carry out your job role

Standards include codes of practice, regulations, minimum standards and national occupational standards (NOS). They have been written to guide workers in becoming competent and providing care that meets the required level of quality. There are different standards for different **job roles** and different **work settings**.

### ACTIVITY

Ask your colleagues and manager which standards you have to follow in order to provide the required quality of care. Give three examples of each in the spaces below and describe how each standard influences the way you carry out your work.

1. Give three examples of codes of practice that you need to follow.
   ✿

   ✿

   ✿

2. Give three examples of regulations that you need to follow.
   ✿

   ✿

   ✿

3. Give three examples of minimum standards that you need to follow.

✿

✿

✿

4. Give three examples of NOS that you need to follow.

✿

✿

✿

# Ensure that your attitudes and beliefs don't obstruct the quality of your work

Our **attitudes** and what we believe to be right and wrong affect the way we behave. We don't all share the same attitudes and **beliefs**, which is why people behave in different ways. For example, if you assume that all older people are incapable of making their own decisions, you might not let them get involved in decision making, or you might make decisions that don't benefit them. Similarly, the behaviour of people holding certain religious or political beliefs can have a negative impact on those who don't share their beliefs.

To be competent in your work role, you must make sure that your attitudes and beliefs don't affect the quality of your work.

 ACTIVITY

Complete the gaps in the following passages using the words below and answer the questions.

stereotype     prejudiced     label

The attitudes and beliefs of health and social care workers affects the quality of their work when they

_____ people according to just one of their characteristics. For example, referring to someone as 'elderly' or 'the diabetic in bed 3' ignores the fact that the person has characteristics other than age or state of health. Workers who label the people they care for and support fail to meet all of their needs.

1. How do you label the people you support?

2. How might labelling affect the quality of your work?

3. How can you ensure that you don't label the people you support?

The attitudes and beliefs of health and social care workers affects the quality of their work when they _____. This means means treating people the same just because they share one or two characteristics. Older people are often stereotyped – it's assumed that because some of them have bladder problems or are forgetful, they are all incontinent or deranged! This is obviously not true and leads to care and support that is unlikely to meet an individual's specific needs.

4. What stereotypes do you use at work?

5. How might stereotyping people affect the quality of your work?

6. How can you ensure that you don't stereotype the people you support?

The attitudes and beliefs of health and social care workers affects the quality of their work when they prejudge people and treat them accordingly. For example, a social care worker meeting a young single mother for the first time might prejudge her to be promiscuous and a benefit scrounger. Such a judgement could be very misplaced, and anyone making that judgement is at risk of treating the person unfairly. We say their behaviour is _____.

7. What sort of people are you likely to prejudge?

8. How might your prejudices affect the quality of your work?

9. How can you ensure that you are not prejudiced in your work?

You should not stereotype, prejudge or label

# Reflect on your work activities

## Reflecting on your work activities is an important way to develop your knowledge, skills and practice

**Your questions answered...**

People at work, my manager and my assessor are always talking about reflective practice. What does it mean and why is it important?

**Reflecting**, or thinking about the way you carry out activities, is a good way to learn and improve your **work practice**. It also helps you get to know and understand yourself better. Everyone working in health and social care should develop a habit of reflecting on their work practice. We call this reflective practice.

Reflective practice involves identifying a work activity and thinking about:

✿ what you have to do
✿ how you feel and what you think as you do it
✿ why you feel and think this way
✿ what's good about the way you carry it out – and what's bad
✿ why you think the way you carry it out is good – or bad
✿ what you could change to make the activity better for everyone concerned.

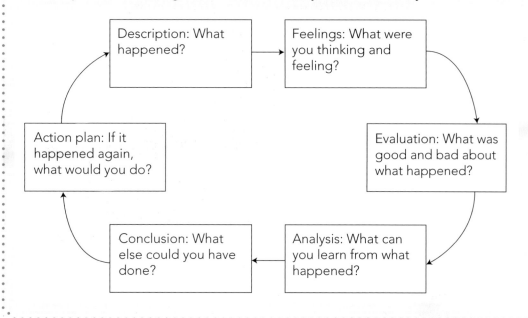

## Rose

 **CASE STUDY**

Ellen works as a domiciliary care worker. This is her reflection after a visit to one of her clients, Rose.

**Description: What happened?**

I visited Rose, who has dementia. Over the past two days, Rose appears to have been more confused than usual, and today she is also sleepy and disoriented. She appears to have slept in the chair and the house is cold. She hasn't eaten the sandwich I had left for her or drunk the hot chocolate in the flask.

**Feelings: What were you thinking and feeling?**

I thought something was wrong but I didn't know what it was and felt guilty that I hadn't contacted my manager for advice sooner.

**Evaluation: What was good and bad about what happened?**

What was good was that when I finally realised something wasn't right, I knew what to do.

What was bad was that there was a delay before I could help because I needed to get advice.

**Analysis: What can you learn from what happened?**

I have learned that confusion is different from dementia and could be the result of an infection, which can be treated. If you really know the client it is easier to spot the small changes.

**Conclusion: What else could you have done?**

I should have realised something wasn't right sooner and talked to my manager, who would have contacted Rose's GP straightaway.

**Action plan: If it happened again, what would you do?**

I would look for signs and symptoms of a possible infection, which was why Rose was more confused than usual.

1. How do you think reflecting on the situation is different from just dealing with the situation?

2. How do you think keeping a record of your reflections can help to improve your practice?

## ACTIVITY

Think about a work activity you do on a regular basis and answer the following questions.

1. Describe the activity.

2. What do you think and feel when you're carrying it out?

3. Why do you have these thoughts and feelings?

4. What is good and what is bad about the activity?

5. Why is it good and why is it bad?

6. How could you change the activity to make it a better experience for everyone involved?

7. How would your work practice improve by changing the activity as you have suggested?

8. What have you learned about your work practice and about yourself by answering these questions?

## Assess how well your own knowledge, skills and understanding meet standards

In order to provide quality care and support that meets the different standards, you need to be able to assess and monitor how well you're doing and be prepared to make improvements!

### ACTIVITY

Answer the following questions about one of your day-to-day work activities.

1. What standards do you need to follow in order to provide care and support that meets the required level of quality? Think about codes of practice, regulations, minimum standards and NOS.

2. Rate the way you meet the standards on a scale of 1 to 5, where 1 is 'Excellent' and 5 is 'In need of improvement'.

3. If you gave yourself a 1, give three examples of why you feel your care and support is excellent. If you didn't give yourself a 1, give three examples of how you aren't providing high quality care and support.

4. How can you improve the way you provide care and support so that you meet the standards? Answer this in terms of your:

✿ knowledge

✿ skills

✿ understanding.

# Demonstrate the ability to reflect on your work activities

 **ACTIVITY**

Keep a diary for two or three weeks to show that you're thinking about:

* the way you carry out day-to-day activities
* how well you carry them out and whether they meet standards
* how you think you could improve the way you work, including what you need to learn and what skills and understanding you need to improve.

You could set out your diary using the following headings:

Date and time

Activity carried out

Which standards you need to meet to do the activity well

How you met the standards when you did the activity

How you didn't meet the standards when you did the activity

What you would do differently next time (if anything)

**Assessor tip**

Use your job description, codes of practice and the NOS as a basis for a reflective discussion with your assessor so you can demonstrate your competence. You will find this easier after a direct observation of your practice by your assessor.

# Agree a personal development plan

## Sources of support for your learning and development

**key term**

**Carers:** people who provide unpaid help and support to, for example, relatives, friends and neighbours.

The activities so far have given you an opportunity to reflect on your learning and development needs. Other people can help you identify what you need to learn and understand, and what skills you need to develop. They include the people you care for and support as they know more than anyone else about how they'd like their needs met! Others include:

* family, friends and **carers** of the people you care for and support
* people within your organisation, for example colleagues, your supervisor, line manager and employer
* people with whom you have a working relationship but who don't work in your organisation, for example your assessor, visiting health and social care professionals and union representatives.

## ACTIVITY

Complete the gaps in the following sentences using the words below to show that you know how different people can support you in your learning and development.

training    feedback    needs    formal    meet    developing    informal

| People | How they can support me in my learning and development |
| --- | --- |
| The people I care for and support. | By telling me how I can meet their _____. |
| Family, friends and carers of the people I care for and support. | By telling me how I can _____ the person's needs. |
| My colleagues and other professionals. | By giving me _____ on how I work. |
| My supervisor. | Through both _____ and _____ supervision. |
| My line manager and employer. | By organising _____ for me to attend. |
| My assessor. | By giving me feedback on how I am _____. |

Different people can support your learning and development

## ACTIVITY

Complete the crossword to show you where else you can get support for your learning and development. The first letter of each answer has been given as an extra clue.

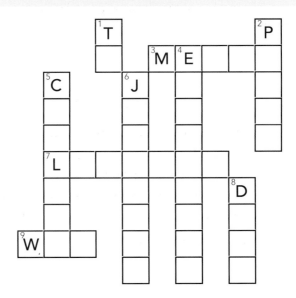

### Across

3. This includes the press, which is a useful source of information (5)
7. A place where you can borrow books, specialist journals, DVDs and so on (7)
9. Another word for the internet (3)

### Down

1. Shows programmes and films, some of which are about health- and social care-related issues (2)
2. Parts of websites or books where you can read information (5)
4. Name of the type of learning an internet course provides (1-8)
5. A place where adults can go to learn (7)
6. Specialist versions of these are a good source of expert and professional knowledge (8)
8. Discs that store programmes, films, training material, and so on, that can be of interest to health and social care workers (4)

# Agreeing your personal development plan and who should be involved

Your personal development plan (PDP) is a plan to show:

* what you need to develop, for example knowledge and understanding of dementia, and communication skills when supporting someone who has dementia

* what you need to do to improve your knowledge, skills and understanding. This would usually be a series of different learning activities, each with its own **learning objective**

* when to review your learning and development to see how well you're doing.

The people who support you in your learning and development are involved in your PDP. Their feedback and suggestions can help you identify your learning objectives, and they are in a good position to monitor how well you're doing. But your ideas and suggestions are important as well. Don't agree to a plan for your personal development if you're not confident you can follow it.

Be smart when planning your personal development by using SMART learning objectives.

**key term**

**Learning objective:** a statement that describes what the learner will know, understand or be able to do as a result of taking part in a learning activity.

 ## ACTIVITY

Complete the gaps in the following sentences using the words below

Specific   Relevant   Achievable   Time-bound   Measureable

Learning objectives should be:

_____, that is, clear, precise and detailed.

_____, otherwise how would you know you had learned anything?

_____. There's no point setting a target if learning's just not possible for you at the moment.

_____, which means your learning objectives have to be meaningful and appropriate to your work.

_____. Set yourself a date by which to achieve your learning – but remember to review your plan and change dates if necessary.

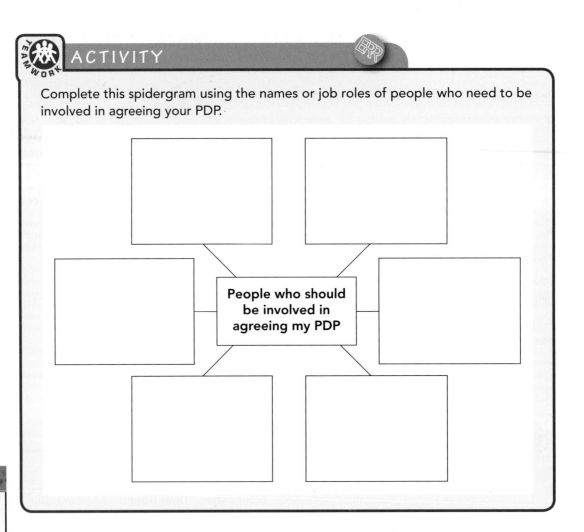

**ACTIVITY**

Complete this spidergram using the names or job roles of people who need to be involved in agreeing your PDP.

People who should be involved in agreeing my PDP

## Drawing up your PDP

PDPs are usually drawn up and reviewed during **appraisals**. You've already identified the people who should be involved in agreeing your PDP. Their feedback and suggestions need to be taken into account when identifying your learning objectives. However, it is during appraisals that learning objectives and dates to review your learning and development are agreed.

**ACTIVITY**

Think of one of your work activities that you would definitely like to improve. Complete the following table to show you are thinking about how to manage your learning and development. Ask your supervisor for feedback on what you've written. An example has been done for you.

| My learning objectives | Learning activities that will help me achieve my learning objectives | When I aim to have achieved my learning objectives | Dates to review my learning and development |
|---|---|---|---|
| To be able to use sign British Sign Language (BSL). | Enrol on a BSL course at my local college. | The course is six months long, so in six months from now. | Two months and then four months into the course. Also two months after the course has finished, to check that I can put my learning into practice. |
| | | | |

Ask your supervisor for feedback

**Assessor tip**

Ask your supervisor if your assessor can observe a supervision or appraisal meeting where you discuss your PDP as this will give you excellent evidence for your portfolio.

# Develop your knowledge, skills and understanding

The following activities will give you an opportunity to show that you are learning and developing at work. It's a good idea to keep records of what you've achieved and learned at work, so that you can use them for evidence in your PDP. The more time you put into reflecting on how you do your work, the more examples you can gather for your PDP.

# Show how a learning activity has improved your knowledge, skills and understanding

You will attend formal learning activities, such as a training course, to develop your knowledge and skills. However, you can also learn and develop your practice through your everyday work. For example, through:

- information about new ways of working that are shared during team meetings
- working with a more experienced team member to learn and/or practise a new skill
- talking with clients, their families and other practitioners about their experience of different medical conditions
- reflecting on your work practice during supervision.

*This was discussed*

## ACTIVITY

Complete the spidergram below to show how a learning activity has improved your knowledge, skills and understanding.

In the central hub, describe a learning activity in which you have recently taken part, such as a training session at work, a college course, reading a specialist journal or following an e-learning programme.

Working clockwise, in the surrounding hubs describe the different things you've learned, understood and can now do as a result of the learning activity.

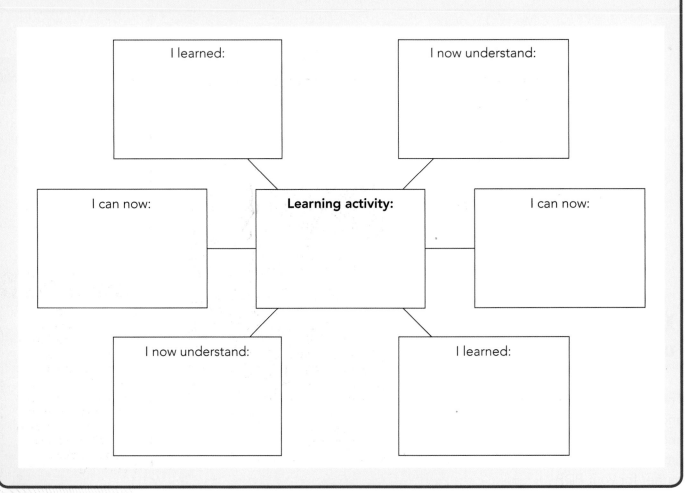

# Show how reflecting on a situation has improved your knowledge, skills and understanding

## CASE STUDY

Dorothy lives in a residential care home. She has Alzheimer's disease and is very confused. Late one night she managed to find her way out of the building through a fire escape door. In doing so, she set off the fire alarm. A member of staff went to check why the alarm had gone off. She noticed the fire door was open and closed it without looking any further. As a result, Dorothy was left outside in the cold in her night clothes, not knowing where she was, until she was discovered missing about an hour later.

It is **procedure** in the care home to close fire doors when the fire alarm goes off. As far as the member of staff was concerned, her job was to respond to the fire alarm by closing the fire door.

If you had been that member of staff, no doubt you would be horrified that carrying out a particular activity – following a procedure – could have such a disastrous outcome.

1. What would you have learned from this situation?

2. How would you change things to make sure that such a situation wasn't repeated?

What needs to be changed to make sure this doesn't happen again?

### key term

**Procedure:** a document that tells a worker exactly how to do a specific work activity.

### Assessor tip

When you have almost completed your diploma, have a reflective discussion with your assessor as this will really help you to recognise and appreciate how far you have progressed, as well as providing good portfolio evidence.

# Show how feedback from others has developed your knowledge, skills and understanding

## ACTIVITY

Follow the instructions below to help you complete the table.

1. Identify three of your day-to-day activities on which you have received feedback in the past.
2. Describe the activities and make a note of the feedback in the table below.
3. Finally, describe how you have used that feedback to carry out the activities.

| Description of activity | Feedback I received | How I used the feedback |
| --- | --- | --- |
|  |  |  |
|  |  |  |
|  |  |  |

**key term**

**Professional registration:** this is a requirement for some job roles in health and social care. To become registered, you need to show that you are committed to professional standards and personal development.

# Show how to record progress in relation to your personal development

When you practised drawing up your PDP on pages 40–41 you were asked to think about review dates. Reviewing is about checking progress – what you've learned, how much more you understand, and what you can do now that you couldn't do before. It's important to record your progress so that you can see the benefits of the PDP process. For example, you can give yourself a pat on the back, back up your application for promotion, show that you use feedback and support, and identify further areas for development. Also, for some job roles it's necessary to demonstrate personal development when applying for **professional registration.**

Going to your appraisal meeting well prepared will also help your manager to understand what you have achieved. If you don't tell them, they might not know.

In your appraisal, your manager may give you some feedback on how they feel you are progressing. This might be based on conversations they have had with colleagues or on their own observations. Take a note of what they say, especially if they identify areas for development. View it as an opportunity to improve, in order to deliver the best quality care.

The next activity gives you an opportunity to think about how to record evidence of your progress.

I am now a qualified signer

 **ACTIVITY**

Complete the table to show how you can record your learning and development. An example has been done for you.

| Aspect of personal development | Evidence to show how I have developed in my work |
|---|---|
| I am now a qualified signer. | ✿ Certificate for Level 1 Award in British Sign Language (BSL). My certificate is in my file in the office.<br>✿ Photographs of me using BSL with Mrs S. The photographs are in my file in the office.<br>✿ Mrs S's care plan, which records that she is much happier now that she can communicate with someone using the method of her choice.<br>✿ I'm much more confident and self-assured because I have a skill that is highly valued by Mrs S and my colleagues. My supervisor has told me that my new confidence has had a positive effect on my work. See my PDP. |
|  |  |
|  |  |
|  |  |

## ARE YOU READY FOR ASSESSMENT?

☑ **Do you know the following:**

☐ 1. The main duties and responsibilities of your job role?

☐ 2. The standards that help you understand what is expected of you in your job role?

☐ 3. How to ensure your attitudes and beliefs don't affect the quality of your work?

☐ 4. Why it is important to take time to reflect on the work you do?

☐ 5. How to identify sources of support to develop your knowledge, understanding and skills?

☐ 6. The process for agreeing a personal development plan and who should be involved?

☑ **Can you do the following:**

☐ 1. Assess your work practice against the standards?

☐ 2. Reflect on your work practice and show how you have used feedback and learning to develop?

☐ 3. Identify sources of support to develop your knowledge, understanding and skills?

☐ 4. Contribute to drawing up your own personal development plan?

☐ 5. Show how a learning activity has improved your knowledge, skills and understanding?

☐ 6. Show how reflection and feedback from others has improved your knowledge, skills and understanding?

☐ 7. Show how your personal development plan maps your progress and practice development?

# UNIT SHC 23

## Introduction to equality and inclusion in health and social care settings

We all have a right to **equality** and **equal opportunities** regardless of our age, skin colour, sexuality, physical and mental ability, **ethnic or cultural background**. Various laws protect our right to equality and equal opportunities. We also have a right to be included in all aspects of our community, for example to use health and social care services and have an education. Inclusion encourages a sense of belonging and of feeling respected and valued for who we are.

Many of the people you care for and support are vulnerable and have special needs. As a result, they may be exposed to unfair treatment. They may not be able to access the same opportunities as less vulnerable people, which makes them disadvantaged. They are also liable to be excluded from their community. Your role as a health and social care worker is to help make sure their rights to fair treatment, equal opportunities and inclusion are upheld.

**You will need to be able to:**
- ❀ understand the importance of equality and inclusion
- ❀ work in an inclusive way
- ❀ know how to access information, advice and support about diversity, equality and inclusion.

# The importance of equality and inclusion

## key terms

**Equality:** dignity, respect and rights for all individuals, whatever their differences.

**Equal opportunities:** making sure that everybody, regardless of their differences, has an opportunity to access resources, such as money and housing, and life opportunities, such as education and employment.

**Ethnic or cultural background:** the behaviours, expectations, language, values and beliefs of the society, group and family in which a person is brought up.

**Diversity:** differences between individuals, for example, culture, race, gender, religion, age, abilities and disabilities, sexual orientation and social class.

## Diversity

Health and social care settings are obliged by law to provide care and support that meets the needs of a wide range of people. Anything else would mean the denial of people's rights to fair treatment, equal opportunities and inclusion.

### ACTIVITY

Use an internet search engine to find out about human rights and freedoms and, in the space below, identify five rights and freedoms that you think are the most important. The Equality and Human Rights Commission website is interesting and, at the time of writing, shows a YouTube clip that brings human rights and freedoms to life. See www.equalityhumanrights.com.

✿

✿

✿

✿

✿

### ACTIVITY

Complete the table to show you understand what is meant by the term 'diversity'.

| Different people | Ways in which they are diverse |
| --- | --- |
| My relatives. | |

| Different people | Ways in which they are diverse |
|---|---|
| The people I care for and support. | |
| My colleagues at work. | |
| The people who live in my neighbourhood. | |

Diversity

## Equality

Equality means fair and equal treatment. You can help ensure that the people you care for and support are treated fairly and equally by:

❁ valuing them as individuals – accept and welcome people's differences, learn from them and enjoy them!

❁ respecting the fact that they are as important as everyone else

❁ making sure that their rights and freedoms are upheld.

**ACTIVITY**

Inequality can occur when people are treated unfairly and in ways that don't value or respect them. Look at the scenarios below. Show your understanding of the impact of unfair treatment by describing how you would feel in these situations.

1. You write a letter to a shop manager complaining about the service you received but you don't get a reply.

2. A job becomes vacant at work, for which you would like to apply. However, the job isn't advertised but is given to a colleague of yours.

3. You've been waiting patiently at the bar to be served but the barman sees a friend and serves her first, ignoring you.

People are treated unfairly for many reasons but usually because of differences in their skin colour, sex, age and ability. Equal opportunities is about making sure that everybody, regardless of their differences, has the same opportunities in life as everyone else and aren't disadvantaged.

## ACTIVITY

Complete the gaps in the following sentences using the words below. This will show that you understand how people who use health and social care services can be helped to make sure they have the same opportunities in life as everyone else and aren't disadvantaged.

dementia   difficulties   disability   health   learning   mental   physical

- ✿ People with _____ _____ may need an education support worker to help them develop their intellectual skills.
- ✿ People with _____ _____ problems may need the support of a social worker to help them find training, employment and housing, and health care workers for therapy and medication.
- ✿ Someone with a _____ _____ may need an occupational therapist to show them how aids and adaptations can make life easier.
- ✿ People with _____ may need the support of appropriately trained health and social care workers to help them with, for example, memory problems, confusion and depression.

### key term

**Community life:** this includes health and social care services, education, employment, leisure facilities and private services such as shops and banks.

## Inclusion

### Your questions answered...

Inclusion is talked about a lot these days, but I don't know what it means. Can you help?

Inclusion is something we should all be familiar with. It's to do with ensuring that everyone is able to take part in all aspects of **community life**, such as leisure activities, transport, education and employment. Being included in community life encourages a feeling of belonging and of being respected and valued for who we are. Exclusion is when people are unable to take part in community life, for example because they're ill, disabled, poorly educated, out of work, in debt, or because where they live is run down or not safe. Being excluded isolates people and can cause mental health problems, such as depression, increases poverty and encourages antisocial behaviours, such as vandalism and drug and alcohol abuse. Children who grow up in families that experience exclusion are said to be deprived and are less likely to be healthy, do well at school and find a job as adults.

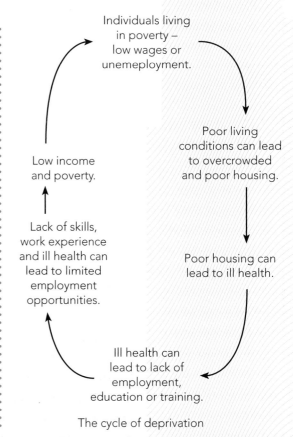

Individuals living in poverty – low wages or unemeployment.

Poor living conditions can lead to overcrowded and poor housing.

Low income and poverty.

Poor housing can lead to ill health.

Lack of skills, work experience and ill health can lead to limited employment opportunities.

Ill health can lead to lack of employment, education or training.

The cycle of deprivation

## ACTIVITY

Complete the table below to show that you understand how being excluded can affect people. An example has been done for you.

| Reasons why people become excluded | How you think this will affect them |
|---|---|
| Out of work. | Less money so less likely to be able to buy nutritious food, pay bills, buy clothes. Could become physically and mentally ill, in debt, homeless, and everything would just get worse. |
|  |  |
|  |  |
|  |  |

## ACTIVITY

Think about three people you care for and support, and who you feel are at risk of being excluded from their communities. Without revealing details of their identity, note down what aspects of community life they are excluded from, how exclusion affects them, and how you can help to ensure that they are included in their community?

✿

✿

## Discrimination

Discrimination is unfair treatment and is usually based on people's age, sex, physical and intellectual ability, size and ethnic or cultural background. We call unfair treatment that is based on these categories ageism, sexism, **disablism**, **sizism** and racism. We have a right to be protected from discrimination.

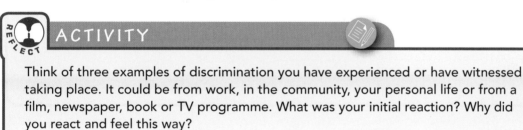

### ACTIVITY

Think of three examples of discrimination you have experienced or have witnessed taking place. It could be from work, in the community, your personal life or from a film, newspaper, book or TV programme. What was your initial reaction? Why did you react and feel this way?

✿

✿

✿

Disablism

## Discrimination in the workplace

You read earlier that we all have a right to be protected from discrimination. This applies everywhere, including in work settings.

Discrimination in work settings takes two forms.

✿ Direct or deliberate discrimination, which is intentional unfair treatment that prevents equal opportunities.

✿ Indirect or unintentional discrimination, which happens when rules, policies and procedures that apply to everyone affect one group of people more than others.

## ACTIVITY

Ask your colleagues and the people you care for and support about occasions when they've experienced or witnessed discrimination at your work setting. Make a note below of an example of direct and an example of indirect discrimination.

✿ Direct discrimination:

✿ Indirect discrimination:

## Practices that support equality and inclusion and reduce the likelihood of discrimination

It's very important to develop work practices that treat people fairly and promote their sense of belonging. Practices that support equality and inclusion protect people's right to fair and equal treatment and ensure that they feel valued and respected, regardless of their differences. How can you support equality and inclusion in order to reduce the likelihood of discrimination?

✿ Be open, friendly and approachable with everyone, whatever their differences. If you find this difficult, ask yourself whether you're prejudiced in some way and whether your prejudices prevent you from treating all people fairly and helping them to feel included. See SHC 22, page 29.

✿ Develop an interest in people's differences, ask questions and listen to their views and opinions. This will help you learn and understand why people behave as they do. Knowledge and understanding dispels prejudices and prevents discrimination.

✿ Don't label or stereotype people. If you do, you won't treat people as individuals. Work practices that disregard individuality don't value or treat people fairly. See SHC 22, pages 28–29.

✿ Follow the bullying and harassment policies and procedures of your workplace. If you see anyone being a bully, politely point out that their behaviour shows disrespect, is unfair and denies people their rights.

✿ Support people who are being discriminated against by acting as their advocate and helping them to make a complaint. See SHC 21, page 8.

# Miriam

## CASE STUDY

Miriam has worked at The Hollies for six months. It is a day centre that provides activities and support for people with mental health issues. For the first few weeks she was quite apprehensive as she found service users' behaviour unpredictable, which made her slightly anxious about approaching them when she wasn't working directly with them. Service users also seemed wary of her.

However, as part of her induction, she attended a training day about mental health, discrimination and how to promote equality and diversity. As a result of what she learned on that day, she returned to work feeling more confident about how to respond to service users as she felt she understood more about mental health and what the service users experienced. Miriam took the time to get to know the service users as people, and to find out about their lives and interests.

She found that service users became more receptive to her and would come to her for help, and with their concerns. During one service user's review, they commented that they valued Miriam's support because she was always ready to listen, to encourage them and didn't make judgements. This made them feel more positive about themselves.

1. How do people behave towards individuals if they lack confidence and understanding about their circumstances like Miriam did?

2. How do you think this makes the other person feel?

3. What behaviours are likely to improve the relationship between individuals?

# Discriminatory work practice

## CASE STUDY

Fairways is a residential care home for older people. The residents have a range of care needs, including those caused by dementia, sight and hearing impairments and mobility problems.

Geraldine has just started work at Fairways. She has never worked in care before. You've overheard her talking about the residents as 'wrinklies', 'cloth ears', 'old bats' and 'psychos'. She shouts at everyone and tries to do everything for them, such as feeding and dressing them. Some of the residents are incontinent and others don't have a good grasp of English. She avoids working with these people because having to change continence pads disgusts her and that 'if people choose to live in England, they should jolly well learn the language'.

1. In what ways is Geraldine's work practice discriminatory?

2. How could she be helped to work in an anti-discriminatory way?

Geraldine's work practice is discriminating

# Work in an inclusive way

## Legislation and codes of practice relating to equality, diversity and discrimination that apply to your work role

Several laws (legislation) are in place to protect service users against discrimination. In addition to obeying the law, health and social care workers must follow guidelines, codes of conduct and codes of practice that are relevant to their job role. These include the following.

- The Equality Act (2006 and 2010).
- The Race Relations (Amendment) Act (2000).
- Human Rights Act (1998 updated in 2000).
- The Disability Discrimination Act (2005).
- The Special Educational Needs and Disability Act (2001).
- The Public Order and Racial and Religious Hatred Act (2006).
- GSCC Code of Practice for Social Care Workers.
- CQC Essential Standards of Quality and Safety 2010.

### ACTIVITY

Find out more about the anti-discrimination legislation and codes of practice by asking your manager how they apply to your work role, and by searching online. Make a list of the most important ones below.

## Assessor tip

Every interaction you have with others should show your assessor your competence in working in an inclusive way, as you should be relating to each person as an individual.

# Interact with individuals to show respect for their beliefs, culture, values and preferences

You read earlier that we're all individuals. This is because we have different ideas about what to believe in, what is worthy of respect, what to eat, drink, wear, read and so on. Good practice dictates that you accept and promote the individuality of the people you care for and support. In other words, you must show respect for their beliefs, values, preferences and cultural background in the way you work with them.

 ## ACTIVITY

Talk to three of the people you care for and support to find out about their beliefs, values, preferences and cultural background. Write about them in the left-hand column of the table below and then complete the table to show how you use that information in your work with them.

| Description of individual's beliefs, values, preferences and cultural background | How I use my knowledge about beliefs, values, preferences and cultural background in my work with these individuals |
|---|---|
| Individual 1. | |
| Individual 2. | |
| Individual 3. | |

# Challenging discrimination in a way that encourages change

Discrimination is not acceptable. Think about your own work practice. Is it always fair and inclusive? It's easy to overlook people's individual differences and needs when you're pushed for time, not feeling too good or the person you're working with is being unhelpful. However, that doesn't excuse your behaviour. The same applies to other people's work practice. Unfair treatment that fails to value people and show them respect needs to be challenged.

## ACTIVITY

Give three reasons why you and your colleagues might treat the people you care for and support unfairly and, for each, suggest how your behaviour should change to guard against discrimination.

✿

✿

✿

## Matilda

## CASE STUDY

Matilda is a 76-year-old woman with advanced-stage dementia who has recently moved into a small residential care home.

According to her family, Matilda has been a vegetarian since her early 30s, when she became very involved in animal welfare. Hakim, one of the care workers, has noticed that in the evenings there is often no vegetarian option left by the cook. This means the care staff have to prepare something for Matilda. This evening, one of the other care workers, Jena, gives Matilda the sausage casserole to eat as the cook hadn't left a vegetarian alternative. Matilda doesn't eat this and as Jena is busy she just takes her plate away without offering her something else. Later, when Hakim is serving the evening drinks, Matilda tells him she is hungry and that she didn't eat her supper because it was meat. Hakim feels he must challenge Jena about this as it is not the first time it has happened.

He shows respect and professionalism by asking to speak to Jena when they would not be interrupted or overheard. He then gives her the opportunity to explain what had happened at suppertime with Matilda.

Jena explains that the cook hadn't left anything for Matilda, that she didn't have time to make anything different and felt that, as Matilda had dementia, she wouldn't notice what she was eating.

Hakim asks Jena how she would feel if she was only offered something she didn't like to eat. She admitted that she wouldn't like it.

Hakim explains that, although Matilda has dementia, they know from her family that she would be distressed if she was made to do something against her beliefs and preferences. After talking it through, Jena begins to see that even though Matilda has dementia, there are still things she remembers, and that what she had done was discriminatory and unfair. She apologises to Matilda and makes her favourite supper.

Hakim also raises the issue with his manager and asks if it is possible to have easily prepared alternatives available for those evenings when they are busy, to ensure that Matilda's needs are met and her beliefs respected.

1. Why do you think it helped Jena to put herself in Matilda's position and think about how she would feel in the situation?

2. How do you think the way Hakim challenged the situation is more likely to help Jena change her practice?

# Information, advice and support about diversity, equality and inclusion

## Where to find information, advice and support about diversity, equality and inclusion

Accepting and promoting everyone's individual beliefs, values and preferences, and making sure they have equal opportunities and feel included, respected and valued can be quite a challenge!

## ACTIVITY

The wordsearch contains a number of sources of help in promoting diversity, equality and inclusion for the people you care for and support. See how many you can find.

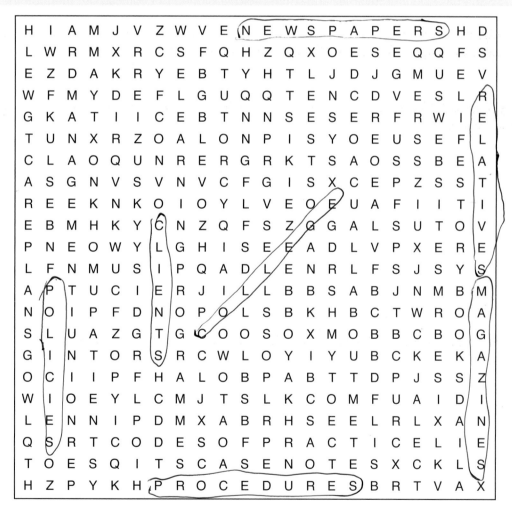

policies   procedures   codes of practice   care plans   case notes   all about me
life story books   textbooks   college courses   learning programmes   clients
patients   relatives   friends   tutor   assessor   colleagues   management
union rep   TV   radio   newspapers   magazines   websites

ACTIVITY

Think about three people you care for and support, and a work activity that you carry out with each, for example helping at meal times or with a personal care activity such as bathing. Briefly describe how you carry out the activity so that you demonstrate respect for their preferences in the way you work. Finally, briefly describe how you found out about their preferences in the way you work. An example has been done for you.

| Person | Describe how you carry out the activity | What information do you use to help you carry out the activity as you do? |
|---|---|---|
| Mrs A. | Helping Mrs A have a bath. Mrs A prefers to get undressed and dressed in private, but likes me to help her in and out of the bath as she's frightened of falling. She prefers to wash herself as far as possible, but loves it when I wash her back! She has favourite toiletries and some special creams to use where she has psoriasis. | Mrs A and her daughters told me about her need for privacy and fear of falling, but her husband told me about washing her back! I did a manual handling course where I found out how to help her in and out of the bath. A doctor advised me about the cream for her psoriasis. Her life history book gave me information about the special toiletries. They're quite old fashioned but you can get them on the internet. I just searched 'old-fashioned soaps' and found what she used as a young woman! She's so happy! |
|  |  |  |
|  |  |  |
|  |  |  |

# How and when to use information, advice and support about diversity, equality and inclusion

Sometimes it is the way in which a society or an organisation is structured that is discriminatory. For example, if an organisation only produces information in one language or in written format, then this discriminates against people who communicate in other ways. This type of discrimination can be challenged through legislation that requires organisations to make their services and information accessible to all.

## Bridge Street Luncheon Club

**Assessor tip**

Planning an activity for the individuals you support is likely to involve finding out about access, disabled facilities, and so on. Keep a record of everything you did to plan the activity, as this will provide good evidence of how to access and use information, advice and support.

### CASE STUDY

You have just begun work as a care assistant at the Bridge Street Luncheon Club. The club provides a social outlet for a diverse range of local people who either live on their own or who are unable to prepare their own meals. The kitchen staff have limited cooking experience and the meals they prepare and serve are the same, day after day after day ...

None of the staff working at the Bridge Street Luncheon Club have received or are interested in receiving any training. As a result, many don't understand their job role. Some have no experience of working with people and have a negative attitude to their work. For example, they are discourteous and impatient and not always clean and appropriately dressed. They also treat all the service users in the same way, regardless of their differences.

The employer, who also manages the Bridge Street Luncheon Club, rarely emerges from her office, where she keeps personal information about staff and service users. She won't let anyone else go into the office because the records she keeps are confidential.

Locks on the toilet doors are broken, there is no running hot water and the steps up into the building are cracked and uneven. There are no security systems in place and there is free access to the building.

There is a growing feeling of discontent with the way that the luncheon club is run, but many of the service users find it difficult to speak up. This is because they lack confidence or have problems making themselves understood. Neither the staff nor the manager have the time or compassion to find out how they feel.

1. In what ways are the service users' rights to equality and inclusion not being protected at the Bridge Street Luncheon Club?

2. In what ways are their individual differences not being acknowledged?

3. How would you try to improve the situation at the Bridge Street Luncheon Club for:

   ✿ acknowledging diversity

   ✿ making sure people are treated fairly and have equal opportunities

   ✿ encouraging a sense of inclusion?

4. How do you think you could get information, advice and support so you could improve the situation at the Bridge Street Luncheon Club?

5. When would you need to get outside advice and support to improve the situation at the Bridge Street Luncheon Club?

How would you improve the situation?

# ARE YOU READY FOR ASSESSMENT?

☑ **Do you know the following:**

☐ **1.** The meanings of diversity, equality, discrimination and inclusion?

☐ **2.** How discrimination may occur, either deliberately or inadvertently, in the workplace?

☐ **3.** How you can support equality and inclusion and minimise the likelihood of discrimination?

☐ **4.** Which legislation and codes of practice relate to equality, diversity and discrimination?

☐ **5.** How to challenge discrimination in a way that encourages change?

☐ **6.** How to identify and access a range of sources of information, advice and support about diversity, equality and inclusion?

☐ **7.** When to access information, advice and support about diversity, equality and inclusion?

☑ **Can you do the following:**

☐ **1.** Interact with people in ways that support their beliefs, culture, values and preferences?

# UNIT SHC 24

## Introduction to duty of care in health and social care settings

Duty of care is about making sure that services are effective and safe. Workers in health and social care settings have a duty of care to the people they care for and support, their colleagues and employers, as well as to themselves and the public. Duty of care applies to everyone in the work setting, including care assistants and support workers in residential settings, supported living projects, domiciliary and day care services, and specialist areas, such as dementia and learning disabilities; health care assistants and support workers in community, primary and acute care environments; and personal assistants employed directly by the people they support or their families

Everyone who provides care and support is increasingly challenged by changes to the way they work, increasing workloads, staff reductions and budget cuts. However, pressure of work doesn't mean you can opt out of your duty of care. In fact, with all these pressures, there has never been a more important time to ensure that the services you provide are effective and safe.

### You will need to be able to:
- ❁ understand the implications of duty of care
- ❁ understand support available for addressing dilemmas that may arise about duty of care
- ❁ respond to complaints.

# The implications of duty of care

## The meaning of duty of care

As a qualified worker, you have a duty of care or a responsibility to provide safe, high-quality care and support to the best of your ability, and to be accountable or answerable for the care and support you give. If there are any reasons why you may not be able to fulfil your responsibilities, you must tell your manager without delay.

If you are a student or trainee, you have a duty of care but the standard of work expected from you is different from that of a qualified worker. In addition, you're not required to be accountable for the work you do until you are fully trained and qualified.

## ACTIVITY

Write your definition of **duty of care** below. Talk to a colleague, your manager and one of the people you care for and support to find out what they think it means. Write all the definitions in the spaces below.

✿ My definition:



✿ Colleague's definition:



✿ Manager's definition:



✿ Person I care for and support's definition:

Duty of care is also defined through the following:

- ✿ Legislation, for example Mental Capacity Act (2005); Control of Substances Hazardous to Health Regulations (COSHH) (2002).
- ✿ Organisational policies, for example those relating to health and safety and safeguarding **vulnerable** people.
- ✿ Codes of practice, for example from the General Social Care Council (GSCC).
- ✿ Practice standards, for example the Care Quality Commission (CQC) Essential Standards of Quality and Safety.

**key term**

**Vulnerable:** someone who has a higher risk of being harmed, for example through catching an infection or being abused.

## Duty of care and your job role

How can you make sure that you fulfil your duty of care when carrying out work activities to meet people's needs?

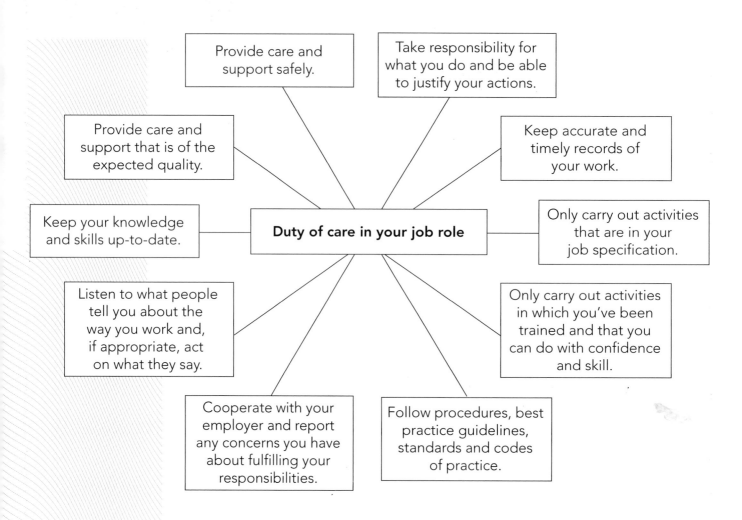

## ACTIVITY

Think about three activities that you carry out on a day-to-day basis. Complete the table below to show how you make sure you fulfil your duty of care whilst working. An example has been done for you.

| Activity | How I fulfil my duty of care |
|---|---|
| Helping at meal times. | ✿ I follow health and safety procedures. For example, I wash my hands and wear personal protective clothing to help prevent the spread of infection, and I encourage the people I'm helping to wash their hands before eating.<br>✿ I complete records for the people I've helped, to say how much they've consumed. I do this as soon as possible, before I forget.<br>✿ I check with the person I'm helping, to make sure they're comfortable with how I'm helping them.<br>✿ I also encourage them to feed themselves as much as they can.<br>✿ I tell the ward sister if there are any problems. |
| | |
| | |
| | |

Safe practice

### Jack

## CASE STUDY

Jack, a porter, has been asked to move a very heavy patient to another ward. When he gets there, there is no lifting equipment to move the patient from the trolley into bed. A nurse says she'll help Jack to move the patient, but Jack is concerned as he hasn't had any training in moving a heavy load without the help of lifting equipment. The nurse becomes impatient and stands her ground, telling Jack that either he helps her move the patient or she will report him for being obstructive.

1. What should Jack do in order to fulfil his duty of care?

2. What might happen to the patient if Jack does as the nurse requires?

3. What might happen to Jack if he does as the nurse requires?

4. What should the nurse do in order to fulfil her duty of care?

Duty of care

**Assessor tip**

Use examples of a real work activity to show your understanding of your duty of care in practice.

## Support available for addressing dilemmas that may arise about duty of care

### Dilemmas that may arise between your duty of care and an individual's rights

The people you care for and support have a right to:

❀ be treated with dignity and respect

❀ privacy and confidentiality

- ✿ make their own choices and decisions
- ✿ remain as independent as possible
- ✿ take risks but be protected from harm
- ✿ be free from discrimination
- ✿ access information that an organisation holds about them
- ✿ be involved in the way their care is provided.

**Dilemmas** can occur when an individual's rights are compromised or denied by your requirement to fulfil your duty of care. For example, your duty of care to protect frail individuals from falling may conflict with their right to take risks by moving about independently. You might think that their behaviour is unwise but they have a right to stay in control of their lives and behave as they see fit. All you can do is point out the risks and be there if needed.

One important factor to consider, when faced with dilemmas regarding balancing rights and risks, is the individual's capacity to make an informed decision – whether they have the ability to think and reason sufficiently to reach a decision. A lack of capacity to make informed decisions may be temporary (for example because of an accident or having had anaesthetic) or permanent (for example owing to an inherited or acquired condition, or failing health). If the situation is permanent, someone may have been appointed to act on the individual's behalf and in their best interests. If the lack of capacity is not confirmed, or is temporary, then you have a duty of care to act in the individual's best interests. That may involve seeking advice and support to enable an objective view of the dilemma to be taken before reaching a decision.

> **key term**
>
> **Dilemma:** a tricky situation.

## Your questions answered...

I'm really worried about an older lady that I support in her own home. She has become quiet and withdrawn and very tearful. Today she told me that one of her sons has taken control over her bank account and, as a result, she has to ask him for money. However, he objects to giving her any money because he thinks she will squander it. She also asked me not to tell anyone or she will be in trouble. I don't know what to do. My duty of care is to protect her from harm, but she also has a right for this situation to be kept private. What a dilemma. What should I do?

Tell your client that you need to discuss the situation with your manager because you're worried and need their help and support. Reassure her that you won't tell anyone else and that no action will be taken without talking with her first. In future, if anyone asks you to keep a secret, tell them that you can't make a promise because there are some things you can't deal with by yourself, especially when someone's health and safety is at risk.

Dilemmas

## ACTIVITY

Using examples from your own practice and/or work setting, complete the table below to show that you understand how conflicts between your duty of care and an individual's rights can cause dilemmas. An example has been done for you.

| My duty of care | Individual's rights | Resulting dilemma |
|---|---|---|
| To only carry out activities in which I have been trained. | To choose how they want to be given care and support. | A service user who is disabled wanted help having a bath but I haven't had any training in how to use the hoist. She was angry and rude because I said I couldn't help her. |
| | | |
| | | |
| | | |

## Getting support and advice to resolve dilemmas

**key term**

**Disciplinary or misconduct procedures:** actions that are taken against someone to punish them for their behaviour.

You read earlier that your duty of care is to provide safe, high-quality care and support to the best of your ability. A failure in duty of care can lead to **disciplinary or misconduct procedures**, for example when failing to protect someone's safety results in an accident or injury. However, fulfilling your duty of care can deny someone their rights, causing a dilemma. Until you are fully trained and qualified, you're not expected to be able to deal with dilemmas on your own, nor will you be held accountable for any dilemma caused by your work. If you have a dilemma, get help and advice.

Your employer is responsible for what you do at work, even your mistakes.

Your manager and colleagues.

The individuals you care for and support, as they are the experts in their care needs.

Your trade union steward or health and safety representative.

Specialist journals and magazines.

**Sources of support and advice in resolving dilemmas**

Organisations that promote the rights of people who use health and social care services.

Support groups and charities that are specific to the patient/service user group with whom you work.

Organisations that promote employment rights.

Experts employed by your local authority.

## ACTIVITY

A disabled woman had her request for a grab rail, to help her walk from her front door to the garden gate and back, turned down by social services because she was frail and might fall while using it.

1. What duty of care was social services fulfilling?

2. What rights was the woman being denied?

3. If you were the woman's care worker, how would you deal with this dilemma?

### Assessor tip

Don't forget that sources of support to resolve duty of care dilemmas can be from within your organisation as well as from external agencies.

Wheelchair users, people with mobility problems and people with sight impairments are sometimes refused admission to cinemas and theatres because they are a 'fire hazard', it is argued that it would be extremely difficult to get them out of a building in the event of a fire.

4. What duty of care is the cinema and theatre management fulfilling?

5. What rights are disabled people being denied in this scenario?

6. If you took someone in a wheelchair to the cinema and were refused entry because the person was a fire hazard, what would you do?

Look back at the three dilemmas you described in the activity on page 72. Where could you go for support and advice to resolve each dilemma and why would you choose this person or organisation?

7.

8.

9.

# Responding to complaints

## How to respond to a complaint

If the way you care for and support individuals conflicts with their rights, they may make a complaint. Complaints can be made, and dealt with, formally or informally. When an issue first arises, it helps to talk. Talking through a situation can help identify the problem and how it can be resolved to everyone's satisfaction.

### ACTIVITY

Complete the gaps in the following sentences using the words below. This will show you know how to respond to complaints.

apologising   calm   encouraging   excuses
feel   interested   listening   active listening skills   understand

You can help resolve complaints by:

✿ _____ people to tell you how they _____ and what is bothering them

✿ _____ to what they tell you

✿ using _____ _____ _____ to show that you're _____, concerned for them and want to _____ how they feel

✿ staying _____; if you stay calm, they'll stay calm – frayed tempers make a bad situation worse

✿ not making _____

✿ _____, if appropriate.

It's important to apologise, if appropriate. If the complaint is about you, but you were following procedures or agreed ways of working, you may not agree with the **complainant**. Explain the situation from your viewpoint and help them to understand why you behaved as you did. If you weren't following procedures, or you didn't take the person's rights, wishes and preferences into account, accept that you were in the wrong and commit to making changes to the way you work. However, be realistic with how you plan to change – don't promise any changes that you can't make. And never make changes to the way you work without first discussing things with your manager.

**key term**

**Complainant:** someone who makes a complaint.

# Mrs Smith

## CASE STUDY

Mrs Smith is very concerned about the way staff at Leafy Lane Residential Care Home support her mother, who has Alzheimer's disease and is very frail. She thinks they neglect her and she has been invited in to speak to her mother's key worker. The key worker is defensive and quick to justify the care being given to Mrs Smith's mother. She constantly interrupts Mrs Smith, accuses her of exaggerating and describes Mrs Smith's mother as a troublemaker who is making things up. Mrs Smith feels that her concerns are not being heard and that the key worker is not prepared to see things from anyone else's viewpoint. The meeting created tension between the key worker and Mrs Smith, and didn't resolve any of Mrs Smith's concerns.

1. How do you think Mrs Smith and the key worker would be feeling as a result of this meeting?

2. If you were the key worker, how would you have conducted the meeting?

3. What might be the consequences of such a meeting?

Responding to complaints

# Agreed procedures for handling complaints

If someone is upset about the care and support received by them or someone else, you should work with them to try and resolve the situation. If this doesn't work, you should encourage them to make a formal complaint. All organisations should have an **accessible** formal complaints procedure that describes exactly how to make a complaint. Complaints are a good way of monitoring how well services are provided and of identifying where improvements need to be made.

## COMPLAINTS PROCEDURE

Sacred Heart Hospital
Somewhere, S1 2SS

### Our commitment to patients

- We will make sure that making a complaint is as easy as possible.
- We will treat your complaint seriously.
- We will deal with your complaint promptly and confidentially.
- We will learn from complaints and use them to review and improve our service.

### When should you make a complaint?

We welcome complaints if you are not happy with the service we provide, for example when:

- you receive a poor-quality service
- you have a problem with a member of staff.

### How should you make a complaint?

Contact the Complaints and Compliments Team:

- **by email** at complaintsandcompliments@shh.co.uk
- **in writing** to the Complaints and Compliments Team, Sacred Heart Hospital, Somewhere, S1 2SS
- **by phone** on 01234 567890.
- **in person** at the Complaints and Compliments Team office at the hospital, which is open from 9am to 6pm every day.

Your complaint will be fully investigated and we will let you have our response within 10 working days. If you are unhappy with our response, you can contact the Chief Executive Jane Fry, Sacred Heart Hospital, Somewhere, S1 2SS.

If you are still unhappy, you can contact the Ombudsman at The Ombudsman, Freepost, London, W1. The Ombudsman will not normally investigate a complaint unless the internal complaints procedure has been exhausted.

## ACTIVITY

Go through the complaints procedure where you work. Make a note below of the main points so that you can give advice in the event that someone asks to make a formal complaint.

## ACTIVITY

### key term

**Parliamentary and Health Service Ombudsman:** this provides a service to the public by undertaking independent investigations into complaints that government departments, a range of other public bodies in the UK, and the NHS in England have not acted properly or fairly or have provided a poor service.

Use an internet search engine to find out about the **Parliamentary and Health Service Ombudsman**'s Principles of Good Complaint Handling. You could search for 'Principles of good complaint handling'. Then complete the following table with the six principles and a brief description of how they apply to your workplace. The first one has been done for you.

| The six principles | How the principles should be applied in my workplace |
|---|---|
| 1. Getting it right. | We must respect people's rights, value their complaints, be prepared to learn from their complaints, and make sure everyone knows what their role is in resolving complaints. |
| 2. | |
| 3. | |
| 4. | |
| 5. | |
| 6. | |

### Assessor tip

You will find it easier if you use real work examples to explain how to respond to complaints and how you use, or have used, the complaints procedure of your organisation.

## ARE YOU READY FOR ASSESSMENT?

☑ **Do you know the following:**

☐ 1. What 'duty of care' means?

☐ 2. How duty of care affects how you work in practice?

☐ 3. The dilemmas that can arise between duty of care and individual rights?

☐ 4. Where to get additional support and advice about how to resolve duty of care dilemmas?

☐ 5. How to respond to complaints using the agreed procedure?

☐ 6. The main points of the organisation's agreed complaints procedure?

# UNIT HSC 024

## Principles of safeguarding and protection in health and social care

There is no excuse for abuse. It is illegal and everyone has the right to be free from abuse. However, because the people who use health and social care services are vulnerable, they are at risk of abuse. As a health and social care worker, your role is to safeguard and protect the people you care for and support. This chapter gives you an opportunity to demonstrate that you understand different types of abuse, what makes a person particularly vulnerable to abuse and what you must do when you suspect, or someone alleges, that abuse is taking place.

### You will need to be able to:
- recognise the signs of abuse
- respond to suspected or alleged abuse
- understand the national and local context of safeguarding and protection from abuse
- reduce the likelihood of abuse
- recognise and report unsafe practices.

# Recognise the signs of abuse

To abuse is to violate or deprive someone of their rights. There are different types of abuse. You need to know what they are, how to recognise them and what can make people especially vulnerable.

## Different types of abuse

ACTIVITY

Use a dictionary or an internet search engine to define the different types of abuse and to complete the spidergram.

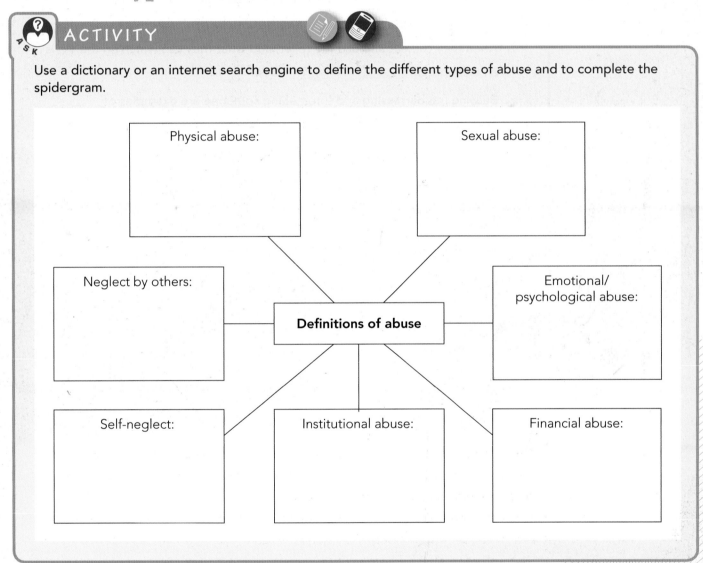

Physical abuse:

Sexual abuse:

Neglect by others:

Emotional/ psychological abuse:

**Definitions of abuse**

Self-neglect:

Institutional abuse:

Financial abuse:

## ACTIVITY

Complete the gaps in the following sentences using the words below.

financial      emotional      institutional      physical
neglect      self-neglect      sexual

- Failing to eat properly, maintain personal hygiene and keep in touch with family and friends are examples of _____ – _____.

- Controlling the way residents in a care home live, for example by dictating when they can eat and use the toilet, and what they can watch on the TV, is an example of _____ abuse.

- Bullying, embarrassing and threatening someone are examples of _____ abuse.

- Failing to change someone's clothes and bedding when they are wet, and not protecting people from health and safety hazards are examples of _____.

- Restraint, hiding medication in food and moving a person roughly are examples of _____ abuse.

- Conning people out of their money or not allowing people to choose how to spend their money are examples of _____ abuse.

- Foul language, unwanted kissing and inappropriate touching are examples of _____ abuse.

## The signs and symptoms of abuse

Signs are things that can be seen, heard and felt by touch. Signs of good health include a healthy skin colour, and blood pressure and pulse rate that fall within normal boundaries. Signs of poor health include pale skin, high blood pressure and a racing pulse.

Symptoms can't be seen, heard or felt. They are the feelings that people have.

## ACTIVITY

The following words can be signs and symptoms of different types of abuse.

| | | |
|---|---|---|
| Depression | Emaciation | Bleeding |
| Loneliness | Soiling | Bruises |
| Scratches | Withdrawal | Anger |
| Burns | Fear | Shame |
| STIs | Unexplained pregnancy | Humiliation |
| Poverty | Despair | Debt |
| Tearfulness | Anxiety | Cuts |
| | Frustration | |

List each word you find under the appropriate heading in the table below. Some words may fit under more than one heading.

| Physical abuse | Sexual abuse | Emotional abuse | Financial abuse | Institutional abuse | Neglect and self-neglect |
|---|---|---|---|---|---|
| | | | | | |

## key terms

**Setting:** a place where people receive care and support, such as a hospital ward or their own home.

**Perpetrator:** someone who carries out abuse.

# Reasons why some people are more vulnerable to abuse

Some people are more vulnerable to abuse than others. Vulnerability depends on the individual and the **setting** or situation in which they live. For example, someone with learning difficulties may be vulnerable because they may not have the experience to deal with a **perpetrator**; an older person living with relatives may be vulnerable because family members may not have the necessary skills and qualities to care for them appropriately.

## ACTIVITY

As you know, bullying is a form of abuse.

Think about situations where you have noticed bullying.

1. Why do you think these incidents occurred?

2. What feelings do you think the perpetrator experienced?

3. What kind of response from the person being bullied would lead to further bullying?

4. What measures would stop the bullying?

What have I done wrong?

## ACTIVITY

Complete the table to show that you understand why different groups of people are vulnerable to abuse. The first one has been done for you.

| Groups of people | Why these groups of people are vulnerable to abuse |
|---|---|
| Older people. | They may not have the physical strength or confidence to challenge someone who abuses or neglects them. |
| People with learning difficulties. | |
| People with physical disabilities. | |
| People with personal care needs. | |
| People living alone. | |
| People with mental health problems. | |
| People living in shared accommodation, for example a hostel. | |

### Assessor tip

When providing evidence about who is particularly vulnerable to abuse, and explaining why they are vulnerable, don't forget to include those people you meet for whom you may not have a duty of care, for example carers or the family of the person being cared for.

# Respond to suspected or alleged abuse

## What to do if you suspect that someone is being abused

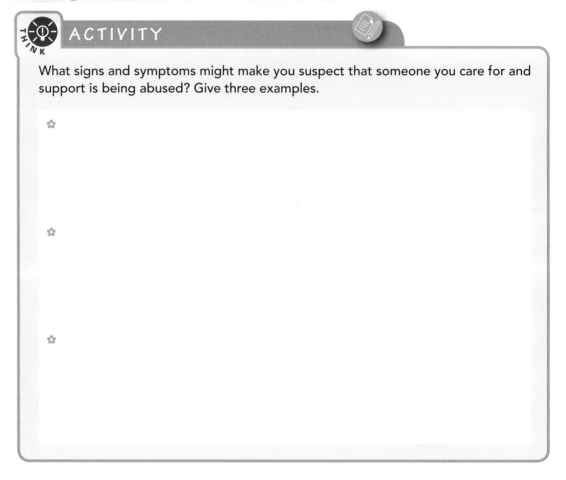

**ACTIVITY**

What signs and symptoms might make you suspect that someone you care for and support is being abused? Give three examples.

✿

✿

✿

If you suspect that someone is being abused, for example you observe an unexplained injury or changes in someone's behaviour that causes you concern, doing nothing is not an option. Don't collude with colleagues involved or make the situation worse by covering it up. Similarly, if someone tells you they are concerned for another person's safety, you must do something about it. However, you must go about it in the right way, and not act without careful thought. You also need to make sure the person is safe before leaving them to report the situation. Your organisation will have a procedure that tells you how to deal with suspicions of abuse, but in general:

✿ **report** your concerns to your manager, verbally and in writing

✿ **never** make a promise regarding an allegation of abuse

✿ **don't** investigate or question anyone yourself.

Your manager must respond to your concerns and let you know the outcome of their enquiries.

## ACTIVITY

Ask your manager how your organisation expects you to respond to suspicions of abuse if the abuser is:

✿ a friend or relative of the person involved:

✿ a colleague:

✿ a manager:

✿ you:

✿ anyone else:

## What to do if someone tells you they are being abused

An effective health and social care worker is someone that the people they care for and support can talk to in confidence. If you are such a person, there may be times when someone will **allege** that abuse is taking place. If this happens, you must follow your organisation's procedure and you should expect to be kept informed about the result of enquiries.

**key term**

**Allege:** to declare or assert.

## ACTIVITY

Ask your manager how your organisation expects you to deal with allegations of abuse. Make a note of what you're told below.

## ACTIVITY

Complete the gaps in the following sentences using the words below. This will show that you understand how to respond to an allegation of abuse.

calm   interrupt   judgemental   listen   record   secret   seriously

❀ _____ carefully to what the person tells you.

❀ Take what they say _____.

❀ Keep _____ and don't be _____.

❀ Don't _____ them; in other words, don't ask lots of questions. Just let them tell you what they want to say.

❀ Explain that you cannot keep what they've told you a _____. Explain that you need to get help from your manager, but reassure them that you won't tell anyone else. Maintain their trust in you.

❀ Make a written _____ of what they tell you, using their own words. Sign and date the record and speak with your manager without delay.

## Mrs Clarke

### CASE STUDY

Mrs Clarke attends the luncheon club where you are a support worker. She lives on her own so enjoys the company, especially yours. One day she tells you very quietly that she can't come any more; she doesn't have any money and, anyway, her daughter doesn't understand why she can't eat at home, because it's cheaper. She shows you her cheque book, which is empty of cheques but the stubs haven't been completed, and she can't find the card she uses to withdraw her pension from the post office. With much anxiety, she tells you that her daughter has been using her cheque book and has taken her bank card, but asks you to please say nothing about this to anyone else as she's sure things will sort themselves out.

1. What type of abuse is happening here?

2. What should you do?

Reponding to an allegation of abuse

## Making sure that evidence of abuse is preserved

### Your questions answered...

Something dreadful happened a couple of days ago at the residential care home where I work – an intruder got in and sexually assaulted one of the female residents. I was the first person to discover the resident after the assault and was so shocked I don't think I dealt with the situation properly. In fact, the police were quite impatient with me. They said I should have preserved the evidence of abuse. I'm not sure what this means. Can you please help?

Your workplace should have a procedure in the event that such a trauma takes place, but the three golden rules for preserving evidence are:

* don't move anything
* don't touch anything
* don't throw anything away.

Because suspicion and allegations of abuse have to be investigated by the police, all associated evidence must be preserved. This includes footprints, fingerprints and body fluids that the perpetrator could have left behind; CCTV footage; records about, for example, the victim's clothing and physical and emotional condition when the abuse was discovered, and any first aid that was given.

## Thelma

 CASE STUDY

Thelma is a resident at a home for people with learning difficulties. It's lunchtime but Thelma hasn't arrived in the dining room. You go to her room and find her crouched on the floor, extremely distressed, and her clothes are dishevelled. She manages to tell you that someone has interfered with her, and you can see that her pants are under a chair and that she is bleeding.

1. What evidence would be needed to investigate whether an abuse has taken place?

2. What must you do to ensure that this evidence is preserved?

**Assessor tip**

If you have been involved in a safeguarding incident you can use this in your explanations as evidence of your competence.

# The national and local context of safeguarding and protection from abuse

## National policies and local systems that relate to safeguarding and protection from abuse

National policies are produced by the government in response to nationally important issues. National policies that relate to safeguarding and protection from abuse, such as Safeguarding Adults (2005), aim to ensure that there is a broad range of services in place to safeguard and protect vulnerable adults.

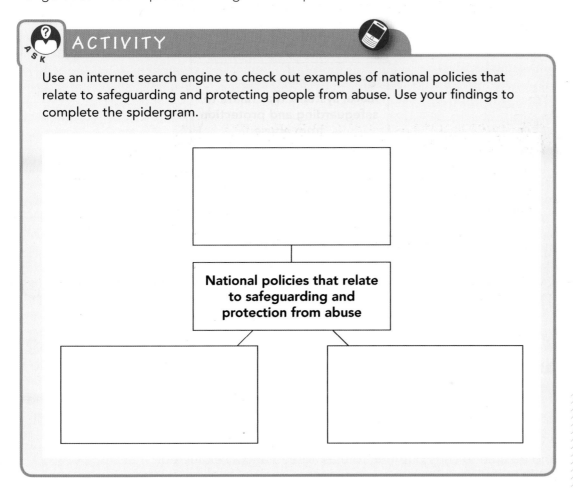

**ACTIVITY**

Use an internet search engine to check out examples of national policies that relate to safeguarding and protecting people from abuse. Use your findings to complete the spidergram.

**National policies that relate to safeguarding and protection from abuse**

Local systems that relate to safeguarding and protection from abuse are arrangements for safeguarding and protecting vulnerable people in a locality. They bring together a range of different **agencies**, for example:

- local health authorities
- local police services
- local authority social services and education departments
- private organisations and charities that support vulnerable adults within a local authority area.

The different agencies work together to safeguard and protect local, vulnerable people from abuse. This is known as **multi-agency working**, and the policies and

**key terms**

**Agency:** an organisation that provides a particular service.
**Multi-agency working:** where a number of different agencies work together with a common goal.

procedures that underpin their work are a response to government policies and the needs of local people.

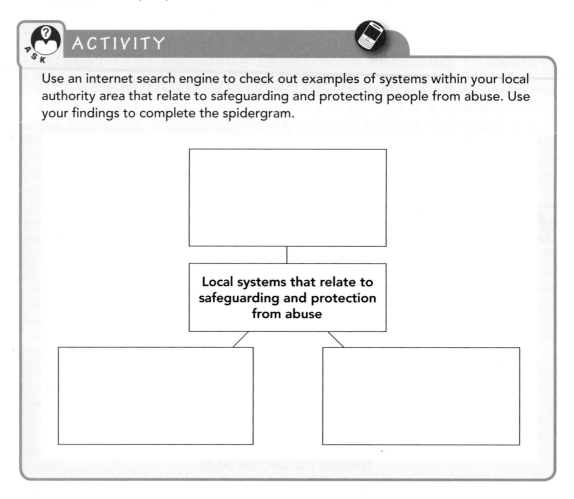

## ACTIVITY

Use an internet search engine to check out examples of systems within your local authority area that relate to safeguarding and protecting people from abuse. Use your findings to complete the spidergram.

**Local systems that relate to safeguarding and protection from abuse**

## The roles of different agencies in safeguarding and protecting people from abuse

If someone is at risk of abuse, workers from different agencies work with them and each other to minimise or to get rid of the risk. For their work to be successful, all workers have to have a clear understanding of their own and each other's roles, and be able to carry out their role as agreed and as expected.

## ACTIVITY

Safeguarding vulnerable adults depends on effective and coordinated joint working between different agencies. Complete the table to show your understanding of the roles of five different agencies in safeguarding and protecting vulnerable adults from abuse. The first one has been done for you.

| Agency | Roles in safeguarding and protecting vulnerable adults |
|---|---|
| CQC (Care Quality Commission). | Under the Health and Social Care Act 2008, the CQC is an agency that makes sure health and social care providers meet government standards of quality and safety. The most recent are the 16 Essential Standards, of which five outcomes are related to the safety of people using services. |

| Agency | Roles in safeguarding and protecting vulnerable adults |
|---|---|
| Local authority social services/ safeguarding boards. | |
| The police. | |
| Local neighbourhood community schemes. | |
| Age UK (formerly Age Concern). | |

# Reports into serious failures to protect people from abuse

The media continues to report serious failures in protecting people from abuse. These failures are usually the result of poor communication between the different agencies, a lack of understanding about work roles and conflict between workers. Government-led enquiries and reports often result from complaints made by the general public or through whistle-blowing procedures (see page 100).

## ACTIVITY

Use an internet search engine to research three cases of serious failure to protect vulnerable adults. Try searching for 'Serious failures to protect vulnerable adults from abuse'.

Which three cases did you research?

1.

2.

3.

What did the courts or enquiry reports say caused the failures?

1.

2.

3.

## Information and advice about your role in safeguarding and protecting people from abuse

There are many sources of information and advice about your role in safeguarding and protecting the people you care for and support. There is no excuse for abuse, so make sure you access information and advice in the event that you have any concerns about your role.

**ACTIVITY**

Complete the following wordsearch to show that you know where to go for information and advice about your role in safeguarding and protecting the people you care for and support.

| | | | | | | | | | | | | | | |
|---|---|---|---|---|---|---|---|---|---|---|---|---|---|---|
| R | Q | Q | Y | C | M | R | J | E | E | I | H | A | Q | E | Y | G |
| B | W | A | G | E | P | M | B | I | U | R | O | G | C | I | L | U |
| A | J | O | B | D | E | S | C | R | I | P | T | I | O | N | S | I |
| L | A | M | C | N | L | E | S | A | S | D | T | Q | R | Q | H | D |
| L | S | L | W | S | S | R | W | E | J | C | H | C | K | N | J | A |
| T | W | J | I | D | F | P | I | Z | A | P | Z | O | P | U | R | N |
| K | L | Z | I | P | M | C | H | R | K | F | P | L | H | L | R | C |
| S | G | J | M | B | I | N | P | P | D | H | S | L | K | G | E | E |
| B | W | G | G | L | R | F | M | D | M | E | Y | E | E | G | U | D |
| T | E | A | O | A | O | Q | K | C | R | L | G | A | G | V | F | O |
| E | G | P | G | S | Z | H | U | U | C | F | M | G | Q | O | N | C |
| X | K | D | E | O | E | X | D | S | G | H | I | U | Y | E | S | U |
| E | Q | D | O | O | E | E | H | T | E | X | Q | E | V | S | I | M |
| Q | O | F | D | L | C | Z | N | T | H | V | J | S | K | K | I | E |
| C | H | J | P | O | M | A | N | A | G | E | M | E | N | T | D | N |
| G | K | L | R | A | A | H | W | D | Z | J | V | T | K | L | X | T |
| Q | W | P | R | O | T | H | E | R | A | G | E | N | C | I | E | S |

policies   procedures   colleagues   management   job descriptions
codes of practice   other agencies   guidance documents

# Reducing the likelihood of abuse

## Working with person-centred values

Working with person-centred values shows that you value the people you care for and support and view them as active partners in their care, not just **passive** recipients of care. As a result, you pay greater attention to the way you provide care and support, which in turn reduces the risk of abuse and neglect.

**key term**

**Passive:** inactive, dependent on others, unwilling to make decisions and choices.

# Encouraging active participation

Working in ways that recognise individuals' right to be involved in every aspect of their life, and that encourage independence, is an important part of protecting individuals from harm or abuse. When ways of working are built around the individual being an active participant in their care and support, rather than a passive recipient, they will be involved in decision making and feel they are listened to. This should make them feel more able to speak out when they are being treated unfairly or in ways that are harmful or abusive.

# Promoting choice and rights

The potential for abuse is reduced in health and social care settings where care workers actively promote individual choice and rights. This approach encourages a culture of listening and openness so that people feel more able to express their views and concerns, making it more difficult for potential abusers to hide their actions.

## ACTIVITY

Complete the gaps in the following sentences using the words below. This will show that you understand the values that are central to a person-centred approach.

dignity   independence   individuals   partnership   privacy   respect

Person-centred care means that:

✿  I must treat the people I care for and support with _____ and
    as _____.

✿  I must promote and support their rights to choice and _____.

✿  I must help maintain their _____ and _____.

✿  I must encourage them to work with me in _____.

## ACTIVITY

Complete the table below by providing five examples to show how you actively promote individual rights and choices in your workplace, and how your actions reduce the likeihood of abuse.

| How you actively promote individual rights and choices in your workplace | How this reduces the likelihood of abuse |
| --- | --- |
|  |  |

| How you actively promote individual rights and choices in your workplace | How this reduces the likelihood of abuse |
|---|---|
|  |  |
|  |  |
|  |  |
|  |  |

**Assessor tip**

A case study that demonstrates how you work in a person-centred way, which encourages active participation while promoting choice and rights, would be a good source of evidence.

## Accessible complaints procedures

Complaints are a good way of monitoring how well services are provided, and of identifying where there are weaknesses, for example the potential for abuse and neglect. An accessible complaints procedure, i.e. one which is simple to follow and openly available, is a good way of reducing the likelihood of abuse as this encourages people to raise their concerns and indicates that the organisation will respond to those concerns rather than ignore them. You can read about accessible complaints procedures in SHC 24, page 77.

## Recognise and report unsafe practices

### Unsafe practices that can affect the well-being of people you care for and support

Unsafe practice may be considered to be any practice that puts others at an unacceptable risk of harm or abuse.

Abuse is caused by:

* poor work practices, such as those that cause pain and suffering, that don't meet people's needs and don't promote person-centred values, choice and rights
* resource and operational difficulties, such as lack of training, lack of time, lack of and/or poorly maintained equipment, lack of appropriate procedures, lack of supervision and security issues that increase the risk of intruders.

## ACTIVITY

Use the following table to describe any work practices and resource and operational difficulties that you think could affect safety where you work. An example has been done for you.

| Work activity | Unsafe work practices | Resource and operational difficulties that could affect safety |
|---|---|---|
| Helping people who are overweight to have a bath. | If someone is too heavy for a worker to help get in and out of the bath, there is a risk of injury to the person and to the worker. | Old and poorly maintained hoists; lack of training in using a hoist; lack of time to use the hoist properly. |
| | | |
| | | |
| | | |

Talk to your manager about your concerns and difficulties.

## What to do if you identify unsafe practices

Unsafe practices must never be ignored. There's no excuse for allowing them to continue. All health and social care organisations should have a procedure for reporting unsafe practices.

### Jim

## CASE STUDY

Jim is the handyman at Carefree Residential Care Home. He sees a lot of things that other staff are too busy or too careless to notice, such as medication left lying around, incomplete entries in the visitors' book, alcohol rub containers left empty for days at a time, spillages on floors, overflowing waste receptacles and staff having to carry out activities for which he knows they're not qualified. In addition, one or two of the staff are not in good health. As for his work, some of the equipment he uses is either very old or in need of a service. However, he doesn't say anything – he gets paid every week and that's all he's worried about.

1. How might these examples of bad practice be considered as abuse? The first one has been done for you.

   ✿ Medication left lying around:
      Health hazard. Physical abuse.

   ✿ Incomplete entries in the visitors' book:

   ✿ Alcohol rub containers left empty for days at a time:

   ✿ Spillages on floors:

   ✿ Overflowing waste receptacles:

   ✿ Staff having to carry out activities for which they're not qualified:

   ✿ Staff not in good health:

   ✿ Equipment past its use-by date or in need of a service:

   ✿ The casual, careless attitude of staff:

   ✿ Staff are too busy:

2. Jim is in a good position to identify bad practice, in himself as well as in others. How do you think he should respond? Give reasons for your answers.

Don't ignore unsafe practices

# What to do if you report abuse or unsafe practice and nothing is done in response

You should be kept informed about how reports of abuse and unsafe practice are dealt with. However, if your employer does nothing in response to your report, you need to speak to a higher authority, such as the organisation that regulates the service you provide. You might even want to blow the whistle (or become a **whistle-blower**) on your employer.

  **ACTIVITY**

1. What organisation regulates the service you provide?

2. What other extenal agencies could you approach for advice and support?

  **ACTIVITY**

Use an internet search engine to find out about whistle-blowing. For example, when should you blow the whistle? Who can you blow the whistle to? What law protects whistle-blowers? What criteria do whistle-blowers have to meet in order to be protected by the law?

## ARE YOU READY FOR ASSESSMENT?

☑ **Do you know the following:**

☐ 1. The definitions of the different types of abuse?

☐ 2. The signs and symptoms of each type of abuse?

☐ 3. The factors that make an individual more vulnerable to abuse?

☐ 4. The action to take, and not take, if you suspect, or a person alleges, abuse?

☐ 5. How to make sure no evidence is lost or contaminated?

☐ 6. The national, local and organisational safeguarding policies and procedures?

☐ 7. The roles of different agencies involved in safeguarding vulnerable people?

☐ 8. How inquiry reports into failures in practice affect safeguarding procedures?

☐ 9. Sources of information and advice about your role in safeguarding procedures?

☐ 10. How to reduce the likelihood of abuse through having an accessible complaints procedure, and working in a person-centred way that encourages active participation and promotes individual choice and rights?

☐ 11. The effect unsafe practices may have on the well-being of individuals?

☐ 12. How to identify unsafe practices?

☐ 13. The action to take if you identify unsafe practices?

☐ 14. The action to take when no response occurs after suspected abuse or unsafe practices have been reported?

# UNIT HSC 025

## The role of the health and social care worker

People who have a passion for working in health and social care play a valuable and important role. Their skills, personal qualities and dedication to providing quality care and support contribute enormously to the health, safety and well-being of the most vulnerable people in society.

This chapter aims to provide you with the knowledge and skills you need to become a safe and effective health and social care worker, to work in ways that are agreed with your employer and to work in partnership with others.

**You will need to be able to:**

❀ understand working relationships in health and social care

❀ work in ways that are agreed with the employer

❀ work in partnership with others.

# Working relationships in health and social care

## The difference between a working relationship and a personal relationship

A relationship is a connection between people. Good relationships are very important as they offer companionship, support, a sense of belonging and a feeling of being valued and cared for.

There are two main types of relationship.

- Personal relationships, for example family, friendships and sexual relationships. Personal relationships involve emotions, so their breakdown leaves people feeling hurt and betrayed.

- Working relationships, for example the relationships you have with your colleagues and the people you care for and support. Working relationships allow you to be purposeful in your work, to give and receive trust and respect and to leave work behind when you go home at the end of a shift. They also protect you by giving you **professional boundaries**.

**key term**

**Professional boundaries:** limits that tell you what you can and can't do in your job role.

  ACTIVITY

Read the following scenarios about relationships and then answer the questions.

- Lena is a care worker in a day centre where her long-term friend, Bessie, has been referred for support. They have been there for each other through good times and bad until recently, when Bessie heard that Lena had been talking about her behind her back, criticising her and spreading hurtful and false rumours.

Friend or professional?

- Tom has multiple sclerosis and Carla is his support worker. Recently, Tom asked Carla if she would help him have a bath. Giving baths is not part of Carla's job role but because they've known each other for such a long time, Carla agreed to help. They ended up kissing.

- Abdul has recently moved into a residential care home. Bob, a care worker at the home, tells Abdul that he knows exactly what his residents are thinking and what they need. Abdul shouldn't worry because if he wants anything at any time of the day or night, Bob will be there to do it for him. He says he is Abdul's friend.

1.  How would you describe the relationships in each scenario?

2.  What problems do you anticipate in the ability of Lena, Carla and Bob to provide professional care and support?

## ACTIVITY

Effective working relationships require the following:

* ✿ clear communication
* ✿ honesty
* ✿ respect
* ✿ cooperation
* ✿ trust
* ✿ reliability
* ✿ shared goals.

Identify which of these factors are missing from the working relationships in the previous activity.

1. Lena and Bessie:

2. Carla and Tom:

3. Abdul and Bob:

# Different working relationships in health and social care settings

Care work involves partnership working or teamwork with a wide range of people.

 ACTIVITY

Think about three colleagues with whom you work. For each one, describe their job roles, how you work with them and what sort of relationship you have with them as a result. An example is given for you below.

I work with the cook. I have to let her know about individual dietary needs and food preferences so she can plan the menu. I have to make sure she remembers which people need help to eat and drink so that she serves their food on appropriately adapted crockery. I have to write the menu up on the blackboard. I have to help her clean the dining room and the kitchen, stack the dishwasher and put the clean things away. I have to help her make orders for food and cleaning materials. We are a good team. We respect each other and get on well but she is senior to me and much more experienced so I have to do as she asks. She likes it when I make suggestions about how we can be more efficient. She says that I use my initiative and am reliable, which is good.

Teamwork in the kitchen

✿

✿

✿

## Agreed ways of working

You need to be able to work in ways that are agreed with your employer and written into your job role.

### Why you should adhere to the agreed scope of your job role

The scope of your job role is the sum of everything you have to do to get your job done. It describes what activities you need to do, how, when, where and who with, and is based on criteria such as your age, capabilities, experience and training. It's important that you work within the scope of your job role because if you don't, you may jeopardise the health, safety and well-being of many people.

## ACTIVITY

Complete the following table to show that you understand why it is important to adhere to the agreed scope of your job.

| Brief description of three of your day-to-day activities | What could happen if you didn't carry out these activities as agreed? |
|---|---|
| | |
| | |
| | |

# Accessing full and up-to-date details of agreed ways of working

Agreed ways of working include:

* formal procedures, which are prescribed, rigid ways of working that you are legally obliged to follow exactly as written
* less formal procedures, which allow for flexibility of working in situations where rigid procedures won't meet individual needs.

## ACTIVITY

Ask your manager what activities have agreed ways of working.

1. How many are there?

2. Which job roles do they cover?

3. What do they have in common?

4. How are they different from each other?

Agreed ways of working with the people you care for and support need to be updated frequently, to take account of changes in, for example, their health and social care needs, medical advances and legislation.

ACTIVITY

Think about one of your day-to-day work activities.

1. What agreed ways of working tell you how to do this activity? For example, moving and handling procedures tell you how to help someone to move from a bed to a chair.

2. If you need reminding about how to do the activity, where can you find the agreed ways of working?

3.  In what situations would these agreed ways of working need to be updated?

4.  How do you know that an agreed way of working is up-to-date?

5.  What could happen if you carried out this activity using an out-of-date technique?

## Implement agreed ways of working

You have a legal and a moral responsibility to follow agreed ways of working, as a failure to do so could jeopardise the health, safety and well-being of everyone concerned. For the same reason, you must never carry out any activity that has not been agreed and written into your job role.

### ACTIVITY

Keep a diary for a week to describe four or five of your day-to-day activities and how you make sure that you follow agreed ways of working. Ask a senior colleague to confirm that you follow agreed ways of working by initialling each entry.

Make sure you follow agreed ways of working

## Lisa

### CASE STUDY

Lisa is a care support worker in a day care setting for adults with learning difficulties. She is still in training but is able to assist her colleagues in most aspects of the work, such as making sure the clients are safe, happy and stimulated. One thing she hasn't been trained to do is support people who've been abused. However, one of the clients, Penny, has told her that she doesn't want to go home because her mum hurts her. Lisa can see bruises on Penny's upper arms. When Penny's mother arrives to take her home, Lisa accuses her of physical abuse in front of everyone and threatens to call the police.

1. Is Lisa implementing agreed ways of working? Explain your answer.

2. What could be the consequences of Lisa's behaviour for:
   ✿ Lisa?

   ✿ Penny?

   ✿ Penny's mother?

   ✿ Lisa's employer and colleagues?

Agreed ways of working?

# Working in partnership with others

## The importance of working in partnership with others

### ACTIVITY

Complete the spidergram below with the job roles of six people with whom you work. Think in terms of visiting professionals, voluntary organisations, and colleagues at your work setting who have a different role from you.

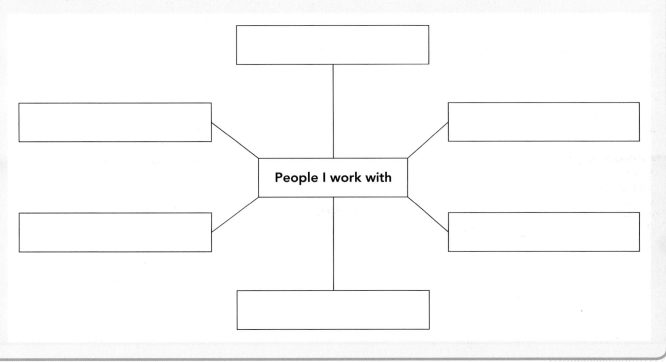

**People I work with**

When working in health and social care, teamwork or partnership is very important. It enables people with different skills and qualities to come together to meet all of an individual's needs. Your work with the people you care for and support is essential, but they may have needs that you or your organisation can't meet.

## Mrs Knight

### CASE STUDY

Mrs Knight, who is in her late 80s, lives alone in her bungalow. Her memory is deteriorating, she has mobility problems that put her at risk of falling and her health is deteriorating because she finds it difficult to look after herself and her home properly. She is also very lonely because her family is not close by and her friends are either dead, have moved to live with their family or are in residential care. She has always been a devout Roman Catholic but can no longer go to church.

Imagine that you are Mrs Knight's key worker. What five organisations would you work with to promote her health, safety and well-being? Explain your suggestions.

✿

✿

✿

✿

✿

Who can help Mrs Knight?

## ACTIVITY

Talk to your manager about the benefits of working with other organisations in meeting the needs of the people you care for and support. Note down the three benefits that you think are most important and explain why you think they're important.

✿

✿

## Ways of working that can help improve partnership working

**Partnership working** in health and social care requires individuals from different organisations to work together with the people they care for and support to deliver a **holistic care package**. However, it is not always straightforward. Different organisations may have different budgets and ways of doing things, and conflicts may arise if this is not taken into account. On a personal level, different people have different ideas and approaches, which can be very helpful at times but, if not managed properly, can lead to disagreements.

## Mr Ibrahim

### CASE STUDY

Mr Ibrahim is having a few days in residential care after a long stay in hospital recovering from a broken hip and shoulder. The manager of the care home is required to put a care package together so that Mr Ibrahim can go home and remain as independent as possible. She has identified several different local health and social care organisations that could be brought together as a partnership to produce a care package to support Mr Ibrahim when he goes home.

- Occupational therapy. This is an NHS service but it is currently understaffed and can't promise to get out to assess Mr Ibrahim for at least a fortnight.
- Physiotherapy. This is also an NHS service but the physiotherapist and the care home manager disagree about Mr Ibrahim's physiotherapy needs.
- Support for you. This is an organisation that employs care workers to deliver personal care to people in their own homes. It has a reputation for employing staff who are not committed and are only in the job for the money.
- Movability. This is an organisation that provides and installs aids and adaptations for people who need help to live independently. They are very difficult to pin down and don't reply to voicemails and emails.
- Spick and Span. This is a new organisation that provides cleaning and laundry services. Their procedures are very rigid and the staff don't have any experience of working with people from different cultures.

Give three examples of conflicts within this partnership that you think might arise in meeting Mr Ibrahim's health and social care needs.

# Avoiding conflicts when working in partnership

To avoid conflicts when working in a partnership, you need to:

* communicate effectively and keep all partners informed about your work
* aviod letting your opinions and beliefs get in the way of meeting health and social care needs; the partnership exists for the people who need care and support, not for you or your organisation
* know and understand everyone's role in the partnership, including your own
* show courtesy and respect for everyone in the partnership, including the people who need care and support
* be flexible and prepared to learn new ways of doing things.

Partnership working

## ACTIVITY

Think about three meetings you've recently attended. Use the table below to explain your contributions to making the meetings go well. An example has been done for you.

| What I did to make the meeting go well | Why my behaviour helped the meeting go well |
| --- | --- |
| I listened to what everyone had to say and didn't interrupt. | It's polite to listen and not interrupt. Listening shows respect for the person who's speaking. It also shows that you're interested and want to understand what they have to say. If I don't listen, I won't get to know what everyone's roles are in giving care and support, including my own, which means I won't be able to fulfil my duty of care. |
| | |
| | |
| | |

# Skills and approaches for resolving conflicts

**ACTIVITY**

Think about a recent meeting with someone you care for and support, or with a group of colleagues, that left you feeling frustrated and stressed.

1. What made you feel this way? Was there a clash of personalities or an argument, or did people behave inappropriately?

2. How do you think the meeting could have been run so that everyone would come away feeling satisfied and in agreement about how to move forward?

There are countless ways of resolving conflicts but the main skills and approaches are to:

✿ find out exactly what caused the conflict and how people feel; stay calm, listen carefully and respect everyone's views

✿ explore different solutions; different people have different ideas about how to resolve a conflict

✿ try the agreed solution. If that doesn't work, try another.

**ACTIVITY**

Use an internet search engine to check for five ways to resolve conflicts. Use what you find on the internet to create your own checklist below.

✿

✿

✿

✿

✿

# How and when to access support and advice

## Your questions answered...

I've just moved to a hospital department where everyone seems to be in conflict. Every meeting I've attended so far has resulted in people quarrelling with each other for one reason or another. At this morning's **multidisciplinary meeting**, a colleague said I was not 'pulling my weight'. I was upset and embarrassed. I'm also angry because I really don't feel I was treated fairly. What should I do?

Everyone experiences problems from time to time in their partnership role and in coping with conflicts. Common problems include not being able to stay calm in tense situations, personality clashes and being asked to do something that is outside the scope of your job role. Deal with the problem immediately by getting help as soon as you can. Sources of support and advice include the people you're in conflict with. Talk things through, tell them how you feel. You could also talk to a trusted colleague, your manager or a union representative. They'll give you honest, objective feedback and advice. Have a look at your workplace's procedures for dealing with conflicts. The last resort is to approach an organisation such as **ACAS**, which acts as a **neutral** third party in resolving conflicts.

### key terms

**Multidisciplinary meeting:** this brings together people with different roles and specialities who have the same aims, for example to provide care and support.
**ACAS:** the Advisory, Conciliation and Arbitration Services www.acas.org.uk.
**Neutral:** unbiased, not taking sides.

## ACTIVITY

Imagine that one of the people you care for and support has started objecting to the way you work with him, even though the procedures you're using have been agreed and are written into his care plan. He is angry and obstructive towards you. His parents are anxious as they want the best for their son. They want you to change the way you work, even though their suggestions would compromise their son's health and safety. At a team meeting, one of your colleagues has suggested that you 'Just do what they want, to keep the peace'. You are worried and are beginning to lose sleep.

1. Who can you go to for support and advice?

2. When should you get support and advice?

### Assessor tip

Care planning and reviews are good sources of evidence of partnership working.

## ACTIVITY

Keep a record of any problems you have when working in partnerships and dealing with conflicts, and describe when and how you used support and advice to solve them. Ask a senior colleague to verify that you access support and advice in a timely manner by initialling each entry.

## ARE YOU READY FOR ASSESSMENT?

☑ **Do you know the following:**

☐ **1.** The difference between personal relationships and different types of working relationships?

☐ **2.** The reasons for working to agreed ways of working and within the scope of your job role?

☐ **3.** The importance of working in partnership with others?

☐ **4.** The skills and approaches needed to resolve conflicts in partnerships?

☑ **Can you do the following:**

☐ **1.** Access current information on agreed ways of working and implement them?

☐ **2.** Work in ways that improve partnership working?

☐ **3.** Demonstrate how and when to access support and advice about partnership working and resolving conflicts?

# UNIT HSC 026

## Implement person-centred approaches in health and social care

We are all unique individuals, with our own life history, preferences for how to live our lives, wishes and needs. The people you care for and support are no different, and meeting their individual wishes, needs and preferences must shape the way you work with them. We call this having a person-centred approach to care. Anything else, such as putting your needs or those of your organisation before those of the people you care for and support, does not result in best practice. The activities in this chapter will help you demonstrate your understanding of a person-centred approach and your ability to put it into practice.

**You will need to be able to:**

* understand person-centred approaches for care and support
* work in a person-centred way
* establish consent when providing care or support
* encourage active participation
* support the individual's right to make choices
* promote the well-being of individuals.

# Person-centred approaches for care and support

## Person-centred values

Person-centred values are the beliefs or principles that underpin work in health and social care.

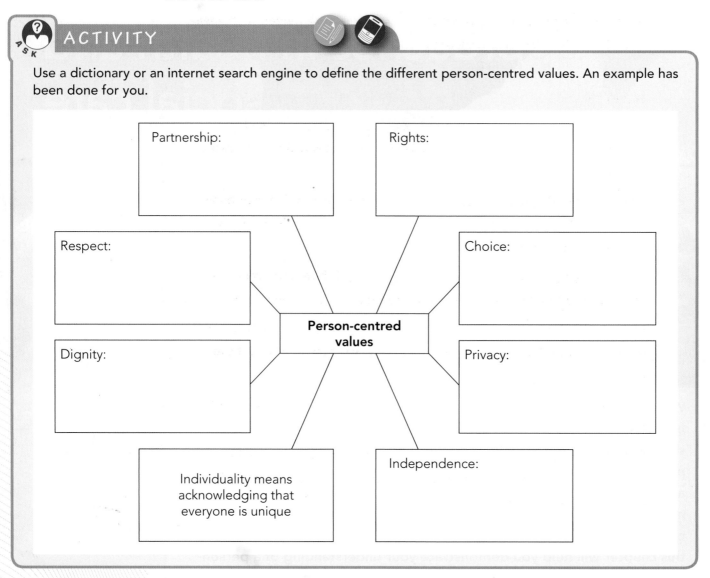

**ACTIVITY**

Use a dictionary or an internet search engine to define the different person-centred values. An example has been done for you.

Partnership:

Rights:

Respect:

Choice:

Dignity:

Privacy:

**Person-centred values**

Individuality means acknowledging that everyone is unique

Independence:

## The importance of working in a way that embeds person-centred values

### key term

**Best practice:** in health and social care, this is safe is high quality care that responds to individual wishes, needs and preferences.

Using person-centred values in your work with the people you care for and support shows that you value them. It is also **best practice**. Person-centred approaches build on the social model of disability. This model suggests that it is the way society is organised that disables people and that helplessness is not an inevitable consequence of disability. An example of the social model of disability is that all public buildings must be accessible to people with disabilities.

## ACTIVITY

Complete the gaps in the following sentences using the words below. This will show that you understand the importance of working in a way that uses person-centred values.

individuals   dignity   rights   respect   choices
partnership   independent   privacy

✿ Acknowledging people's personal preferences, wishes and needs in the way I care for them shows that I value them as _____.

✿ By promoting their _____ I help people to feel valued and important.

✿ By encouraging people to make their own _____ and decisions, I show that I value their opinions about the way they wish to lead their lives.

✿ By respecting people's _____, I show that I value their need for confidentiality and space for themselves, and that it is a privilege to share their personal information.

✿ By encouraging people to be _____, I show that I value them for what they can do and the responsibility they have for themselves.

✿ By respecting people's _____ and helping them to stay proud of themselves, I show that I value them for the way they want to behave and be seen.

✿ By showing people _____, I show that I value them for who they are.

✿ By working in _____ with people, I show that I value their input into the way I meet their needs and want them to remain as much in control as they are able.

## Risk taking as part of a person-centred approach

Everybody has a right to take **risks** and, as you know, promoting people's rights is a person-centred value – it helps people feel valued and important. But risk taking can have disastrous outcomes. Your role is to support people's right to take risks but also to protect them from harm. Acceptable risks are those that are reasonable and fair, and unlikely to harm the person taking the risk. Unacceptable risks are those that are likely to put the risk taker in danger.

## ACTIVITY

Read the following scenarios. What are the risks? How can you help protect the people involved from harm?

1. Craig, 40, who is in hospital with chronic heart disease and has an intravenous infusion, wants to go outside for a cigarette.

   ✿ What are the risks?

   ✿ How can you protect him?

2. Elsie, aged 84, is ready for discharge from hospital after breaking her hip. She wants to go home to her flat, where she lives alone.

   ✿ What are the risks?

   ✿ How can you protect her?

3. Julie, who has Down's syndrome, wants to go to town to celebrate her 18th birthday.

   ✿ What are the risks?

   ✿ How can you protect her?

Protection from harm

# How using care plans contributes to working in a person-centred way

**Care plans or support plans** are documents that record people's needs and explain how, where, when and by whom their needs are going to be met. They are individual to the person for whom they are written. The caring activities they describe must centre on the person involved and their preferences for how care is given. Care plans are not written to meet the needs of the organisations or workers delivering the care.

The care plan should reflect the individual's involvement in the process, as well as those people who are important to the individual. The care plan should be about the individual's life and just services, by reflecting what is possible and not just what is available.

  **ACTIVITY**

Complete the gaps in the following sentences using the words below. This will show that you know the principles of a person-centred care plan.

beliefs **interventions** reviewing timescales support
important preferences likes **outcome** needs capabilities

A person-centred care plan will contain the following information.

✿ The individual's assessed _____ from their perspective.

✿ Their current _____.

✿ The individual's rights, choices and _____.

✿ The individual's values and _____.

✿ The individual's views, strengths, interests, _____ and dislikes.

✿ The things that are _____ to the individual.

✿ What they want their life to be like as a result of support (the desired _____).

✿ The different types of support or _____.

✿ _____ for implementing and _____ the plan.

✿ The things the individual can do, their _____.

Care plans must centre on the person involved

## Ahmad

**CASE STUDY**

Ahmad is 80 and lives alone. He's losing his sight, his ability to look after himself and any desire to stay in touch with people. He's also losing his ability to make decisions and speak up for himself. A social worker has assessed his needs and written a care plan. She hasn't discussed it with Ahmad as she doesn't have time for his dithering. The care plan requires: a social care worker to visit three times a day, whenever he or she can, to deal with his personal care needs; Meals on Wheels to deliver all his food; someone from a local Help at Home organisation to tidy up his flat and bring in items of shopping that they think he will need; and a local charity to send in a befriender to pass time with him and keep him informed of news that will be of interest to him. In other words, her care plan makes sure that his every need is met. She very proudly writes the same care plan for all her 'dear old biddies'. But Ahmad is not happy.

1. Is this *really* best practice? In what way does the care plan fail to deliver person-centred care?

2. Why is Ahmad not happy?

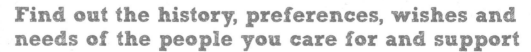

# Work in a person-centred way

## Find out the history, preferences, wishes and needs of the people you care for and support

As you know, everyone is unique, with their own life history, preferences, wishes and needs. Good practice requires that you get to know the history, preferences, wishes and needs of the people you care for and support, because only by knowing them well can you meet their needs appropriately.

## ACTIVITY

There are various sources you can use to find out about an individual's history, preferences, wishes and needs. Complete the wordsearch to show that you know where to go for information.

```
O P B N R M E M O R Y B O X E S Y
G X D E U Z I J V F Z H S S E B M
F A M I L Y T R E E S L M S Z N L
R D O G C Y I F F R I E N D S A L
P V E H R K S W A X Y A T J U Y W
R O D B C F A I T H L E A D E R S
O C T O S X V I U P H K I S O R X
F A U U Q S W P E H V V I N W M S
E T M R M T Z R J J I C N G B F W
S E W S B L A R U D W W A O F S Y
S S N Z D C V B N A M Q T C U A E
I C O M M U N I T Y L E A D E R S
O R H E B Z E F A M I L Y N O J O
N J G L U H L V W D H E S J T I N
A P H O T O G R A P H S N U Y K N
L E W H L H C O L L E A G U E S U
S M A N A G E M E N T Y N O X G S
```

care plans   the individual   family   friends   neighbours   advocates
colleagues   management   professionals   community leaders
faith leaders   memory boxes   photographs   family trees

# Use person-centred values in your day-to-day work, taking into account people's history, preferences, wishes and needs

You need to be able to demonstrate that you use person-centred values in your work with people and that their history, preferences, wishes and needs shape the way you work.

## ACTIVITY

Think about three people you care for and support. Complete the following table to show:

❀ that you know their histories, preferences, wishes and needs, and use them in the way you carry out activities

❀ the person-centred values you use.

An example has been done for you.

| Person (remember confidentiality) | An activity you carry out with them and the need it meets | One aspect of their life history that affects how you meet their needs | A wish they have about how you carry out the activity | A preference they have about how you carry out the activity |
|---|---|---|---|---|
| Mrs B. | I help Mrs B to eat. She has Parkinson's and sometimes the tremors make it difficult for her to get food to her mouth. This is working in partnership, encouraging her to be as independent as possible and promoting her basic right to eat. | She was brought up to use a napkin so I always make sure she has one. This shows respect for the things she thinks are important and promotes her dignity. | She wishes she didn't have to be fed so I am very sensitive and discreet. This respects her dignity. | She prefers to eat slowly so I have to make sure I have plenty of time and don't rush her. This acknowledges her individuality and respects her choice. |
| | | | | |
| | | | | |
| | | | | |

# Establish consent when providing care or support

## The importance of establishing consent

### ACTIVITY

Discuss with your colleagues how you would feel if your dentist removed a couple of your teeth without discussing things with you, or if you went to see your doctor about a very embarrassing issue and he or she called a couple of students to examine you without checking whether you minded? Angry? Powerless? And what about your dignity and privacy?

### Your questions answered...

I keep hearing the expression 'consent in health and social care settings'. What exactly does it mean?

Before you carry out any health or social care activity or procedure, the person involved has to agree to it and their agreement must be based on their knowledge and understanding of what you intend to do. We call this giving **informed consent**.

If they've already given informed consent to an activity or procedure, you should check that they continue to agree. It may be that all you have to say is 'Would you like me to …?' or 'Do you need help with … today?' Don't assume that consent remains in place. People's ability to understand changes and they forget things. Always check.

Some people don't have the **capacity** to give informed consent because, for example, they're very young or they have learning difficulties. In such cases, another, appropriate person should be asked to give consent on their behalf.

It's very important to get informed consent. If, for example, you carry out an activity or procedure without someone's agreement, you could be accused of physical abuse.

**Assessor tip**

You will find it easier to explain person-centred approaches if you show your assessor a care plan you have contributed to, and talk through how you supported the individual during the process.

**key terms**

**Informed consent:** agreeing to an activity or procedure being carried out based on the knowledge and understanding of that activity or procedure.
**Capacity:** having the mental ability to fully understand what you're told, make a decision based on that understanding, remember the decision and tell it to someone else.

Informed consent is one type of consent. There are three other types.

* Implied consent: when the person's actions give the impression that they are consenting, for example attending the Accident and Emergency department of a hospital for treatment.
* Continued consent: when consent continues during the course of treatment, care or support.
* Consent by proxy: if the person is unable to give consent, decisions can be made by an appropriate person, for example their next of kin or advocate.

The capacity to consent means the individual is able to:

* fully understand the information that relates to the decision to be made
* retain that information long enough to make a decision
* make sense of the information and reach a decision, that is can understand the positives and negatives
* express their decision to others.

The capacity to consent can change as a result of the individual's medical condition, and this also needs to be considered.

## ACTIVITY

Think of three activities or procedures that you carry out on a day-to-day basis and for which you need informed consent. What are they and what might happen if you didn't establish that it is acceptable for you to carry them out? An example has been done for you.

* Helping people to use the toilet. If I don't get their permission, they could accuse me of invading their privacy, not respecting their dignity and of physical, even sexual, abuse.

*
*
*

## ACTIVITY

Ask your manager about your organisation's procedure for gaining consent and why you must follow it exactly.

## Establishing consent

 ACTIVITY

Make a note of two activities you carry out that require you to obtain consent. For each activity, indicate how you established consent.

✿ Do the people concerned simply **comply** with the activity, for example by letting you remove their clothes to get ready for bed?

✿ Do they give you verbal consent, such as saying it's acceptable for you to carry out the activity or procedure?

✿ Do you have to get them to give their consent in writing, by filling in a special consent form?

✿ Do you have to ask someone to give consent on their behalf?

Ask the people concerned to verify that you obtained their consent by initialling your record.

Establishing consent

**key term**

**Comply:** to conform, obey or submit to something.

## Steps to take if consent cannot be readily established

The people you care for and support have a right to withhold consent to an activity or procedure. They also have a right to change their minds about giving consent at any time. Some people find it difficult to give consent, perhaps because they have a limited understanding or are too ill. If someone withholds, withdraws or is not able to give consent and you think this puts health, safety and well-being at risk, speak to your manager. It is not your role to try to influence anyone.

**Assessor tip**

You can show your assessor how you establish consent by ensuring you explain what you are doing when supporting individuals and checking they are happy with what you plan to do before carrying on.

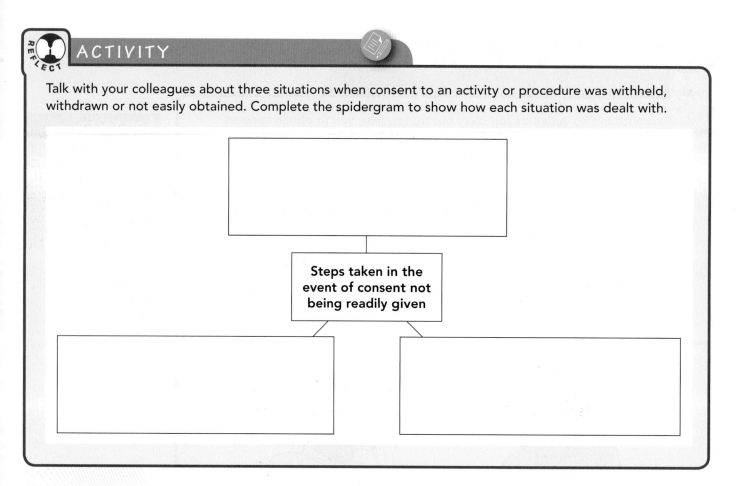

ACTIVITY

Talk with your colleagues about three situations when consent to an activity or procedure was withheld, withdrawn or not easily obtained. Complete the spidergram to show how each situation was dealt with.

Steps taken in the event of consent not being readily given

# Encourage active participation

## The benefits of active participation

Everyone has a right to take part in everyday activities and relationships as independently as they can. Active participation is a way of working that encourages people to remain independent and sociable for as long as possible. It also encourages them to be active partners in their care and support. Active partners have a say in the way their care and support is given and a responsibility to help you in your work with them and to share the load.

You benefit from partnership working as it's an opportunity to improve your knowledge about people, which in turn improves your person-centred care skills. Also, a problem shared is a problem halved; in other words, sharing the work involved in an activity reduces your workload.

## ACTIVITY

Complete the gaps in the following sentences using the words below. This will show that you know the benefits of active participation.

choice   confidence   control   dignity   independent
individuals   privacy   responsible   right   self-esteem

Encouraging the people I care for and support to be active partners shows that I:

❁ respect their _____ to be involved in their own care and to have a say in how it's provided

❁ value them as _____, want to be with them and want to get to know them; this helps build their _____ and _____ – _____

❁ respect and value their need to stay _____; this helps them stay _____ for themselves

❁ respect their _____ about the way their care and support is given; this helps them maintain _____ over their own lives

❁ want to know when they need _____ and how to promote their _____.

Encouraging independence through active participation

## Barriers to active participation

The opposite of an active partner is a passive recipient of care. Many of the people you care for and support will be unable or choose not to participate in their care and support. They may, for example, be too ill, lack confidence, be frightened, not understand what you want them to do or not want to work with you. We call these barriers to active participation.

## ACTIVITY

Think about three people you care for and support and who can't – or won't – participate in their own care or support. Complete the table to show you understand the barriers that prevent them being active partners. An example has been done for you.

| Person (remember confidentiality) | Example of an activity in which they can't or won't participate | Barriers to active participation |
|---|---|---|
| Mr J. | Walking. | He fell recently and has lost confidence. He's afraid of falling again and of the pain and humiliation. He's also quite depressed and has lost the motivation to stay independent. |
|  |  |  |

| Person (remember confidentiality) | Example of an activity in which they can't or won't participate | Barriers to active participation |
|---|---|---|
|  |  |  |
|  |  |  |

There may also be barriers to active participation relating to the care setting, organisation or care worker. For example, the setting may not have the right equipment, the organisation may lack the resources or skilled staff required for support, or individual care workers may lack commitment to active participation or not have the patience and creativity required. None of these reasons are related to the recipient of the care, but they still prevent that person from receiving the help and support they need.

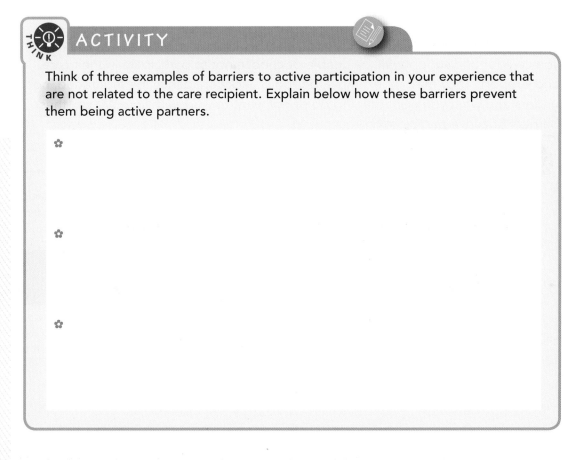

## ACTIVITY

Think of three examples of barriers to active participation in your experience that are not related to the care recipient. Explain below how these barriers prevent them being active partners.

✿

✿

✿

# Ways to reduce barriers and encourage active participation

Being able to participate in everyday activities and develop relationships is a basic human need. Barriers to active participation deprive people of their well-being and damage their confidence and self-esteem. People who are no longer able to join in or do anything for themselves often face the future with hopelessness.

## Edith

**CASE STUDY**

Edith, aged 85, lives with her daughter. She had a major stroke five years ago, which left her partially paralysed. Since the stroke, she has become increasingly dependent on her daughter and now no longer wants to do anything for herself. She has no confidence or self-esteem, she finds it difficult to make conversation so has no enthusiasm for seeing anyone else and because of her mobility problems, only leaves her room to go to the toilet. Edith's daughter despairs for her mum, whose only wish is to die.

Imagine that you work for the Stroke Association, and have been asked by Edith's daughter to talk to Edith, to try to help improve a situation which is doing neither of them any good.

1. What barriers do you think might be preventing Edith from active participation in:

✿ daily activities?

✿ relationships?

✿ her own care and support?

2. How do you think you could help Edith overcome these barriers?

## ACTIVITY

Look back at the activity at the bottom of page 131, where you identified barriers that prevent three people from participating in their care or support.

What can you do to help overcome these barriers and encourage active participation? Complete the space below with your suggestions. An example has been done for you.

How I can help reduce barriers and encourage active participation:

Mr J. Make sure I walk with him, even when he's using his frame, to reassure him that he won't fall and build his confidence

Person 1:

Person 2:

Person 3:

**Assessor tip**

Being observed by your assessor supporting an individual during an activity they identified on their care plan, will enable you to demonstrate how you encourage active participation. Think about how the same activity could be passive for the individual and what actions you should take to ensure these issues are overcome.

# The right to make choices

## Support people to make informed choices

You can only make an informed choice when you know and understand all the necessary information. If you are being asked to make an informed choice, for example between having a local and a general anaesthetic, you would need:

* unbiased, up-to-date, factual information about both procedures
* information from a source you can trust to be accurate and reliable
* the information to be in a language you can understand
* an opportunity to ask questions and check your understanding
* time in which to make the choice that is right for you. A choice made in haste may be regretted later.

## ACTIVITY

Use an internet search engine to find out about Choose and Book, the national electronic referral that gives NHS patients a choice about their outpatient appointment. Make some notes about the service below, so that you can help the people you care for and support to understand what it is all about.

The people you care for and support might find it difficult to make an informed choice, even when they have all the necessary information. How can you help them?

## ACTIVITY

Imagine that your doctor wants to refer you to a specialist. You have been told to make your appointment through the Choose and Book service. What information would you need to make an informed choice about where and when to go?

### Your questions answered...

My aunt is quite old and can't look after herself any more. She's not ill or disabled but she's very weary and needs help. I'm her only relative but I live 100 miles away so I can't do much for her. We think the best option for her would be to go into residential care but we don't know how to choose a home as there are so many. She is quite well off so she wouldn't need any financial help.

I agree about residential care for your aunt but she has to be the one to choose a home. First of all, discuss whether she'd like to live near you or stay in her present location. Talk with her about what care and support she wants and needs. Help her obtain brochures of the homes in her chosen location to see whether they're registered to meet her needs and would support her in the way she wants. Take her to visit the homes she likes the best. You say your aunt is quite well off but help her to check the fees and whether they will cover everything that she thinks she'll want. When you visit, talk to the residents, find out how they feel about the care and support they're given. Talk to the staff to find out if they have a caring attitude, if they are well trained and if they use person-centred values in their work. You could also look at the Care Quality Commission's website to see how it rates the homes she likes best. If making a choice remains difficult, search the internet for organisations especially set up to help people in your aunt's situation.

Choosing a care home is difficult and people need as much help as possible to make an informed choice.

## ACTIVITY

The UK has an ageing population and more and more people need to consider moving into residential care or nursing homes. Use an internet search engine to check for yourself how easy – or difficult – it is for older people to make an informed choice. Try searching with the phrase 'Choosing a care home'.

## ACTIVITY

Think about an occasion when you helped someone you care for and support to make an informed choice.

1. Why did they have difficulty in making an informed choice?

2. How did you help them make their choice?

# Risk assessment processes that support people's right to make choices

The risk assessment process is a careful examination of what could cause harm, whether there are enough precautions in place to prevent harm and what more can be done to prevent harm.

You and the people you care for and support have a right to be protected from harm, so risk assessments are very important. The people you care for and support also have a right to take risks; indeed, some of their choices may contain an element of risk.

**ACTIVITY**

Think of three risky choices that people – including you, your colleagues and the people you care for and support – can make, and indicate what harm can come from each one. An example has been done for you.

✿ Illegal use of drugs. This can affect your physical and mental health, it can break up relationships and can result in a prison sentence.

✿

✿

✿

Risky choices should be backed up by a risk assessment so that the likelihood of harm is either prevented or reduced to an absolute minimum. Risk assessments also enable people to do what they want to do without harm. Your organisation will have procedures that tell you how to protect someone whose choices pose a risk of harm.

**ACTIVITY**

Keep records to show that when the people you care for and support make choices that pose a risk, you follow risk assessments to protect everyone involved from harm. Ask a senior colleague to verify that you follow risk assessments by initialling your records.

## Why your personal views must not influence an individual's choices

We're all unique and it's our uniqueness that allows us to make the personal choices that are right for us. For this reason, we should never try talking others into making a choice that we think is best for them or that best suits our purposes. Help the people you care for and support to make informed choices, ones that are right for them, but don't tell them what you think they should choose. One way to remain impartial is to think about only the facts, rather than the feelings, involved. There may also be legislation or codes of practice that people can refer to in order to make an informed choice.

### ACTIVITY

Think of an occasion when you were prevented from making a choice on your own and, instead, someone talked you into something you wouldn't otherwise have chosen.

1. What was the person's purpose in influencing your choice?

2. Why did you let the person influence you?

3. Was the choice right for you?

4. How did you feel?

Now think about an occasion when you influenced someone you care for and support into making a particular choice.

5. What was your purpose in influencing that person's choice?

6. What was it about the person that enabled you to influence the choice made?

7. Was the choice right for the person?

8. How do you think the person felt?

## Supporting people to question or challenge other people's decisions concerning them

While the majority of health and social care workers use person-centred values in their work, many, for one reason or another, fail to promote the right to choice.

 **ACTIVITY**

Complete the gaps in the following sentences using the words below. This will show that you understand why health and social care workers may make decisions on behalf of the people they care for and support.

best   busy   control   respect   power   preferences   right   value

✿ They have no _____ for people's _____ to make their own choices.

✿ They don't _____ people's personal _____ and wishes.

✿ They are too _____ to wait for people to make a decision.

✿ They think they know what is _____ for everyone.

✿ They like to be in _____ and think that making decisions for people gives them

_____.

People who use health and social care services are often vulnerable in some way. When decisions are made for them, without their involvement, they may feel too frightened to question the decision and may not have the confidence to challenge the decision makers. Your role is to help people question or challenge decisions made on their behalf.

## Stephen

### CASE STUDY

Stephen, aged 19, has moderate learning difficulties. He has trouble learning new things, understanding instructions and maintaining relationships, but he can look after his personal care and everyday needs quite independently. He lives in supported accommodation and works in a garden centre three days a week, where he enjoys tending the plants and maintaining the beds. He's been called to a meeting with his social worker who tells him that they are moving him to a garage to work, as the experience will be good for him. He is devastated and angry that he wasn't consulted but he's unable to express his feelings. Describe three ways that you could support Stephen to question or challenge this decision.

Making the right choice

✿

✿

✿

# Promoting individuals' well-being

## The link between well-being, identity and self-esteem

Well-being is to do with how well we feel about ourselves and how satisfied we are with our lives and what we've achieved.

### ACTIVITY

Unscramble the following anagrams to show your understanding of what is meant by the term 'well-being'. The first one has been done for you.

RSILAPIUT <u>SPIRITUAL</u> well-being is the sense of peace and contentment we develop when we're able to appreciate our experiences and relationships and understand how they affect our values, our beliefs and the way we behave.

OAEMITNLO _____ well-being is the sense of peace and contentment we develop when we're able to understand and handle our own emotions.

ULLCRTUA _____ well-being is the sense of peace and contentment we develop when we're able to participate in activities and hold beliefs that are important to the customs and traditions of the group to which we belong.

OLISRGIEU _____ well-being is the sense of peace and contentment we develop when we're able to hold and express our religious beliefs in the way we wish.

ISLCOA _____ well-being is the sense of peace and contentment we develop when we're able to start and maintain mutually satisfying relationships with other people, as well as enjoying our own company.

LOPCTIAIL _____ well-being is the sense of peace and contentment we develop when we're able to take part in public affairs that affect our communities.

Identity is to do with the way we and others perceive us; self-esteem is to do with how much we value ourselves. It can develop through our comparison of ourselves with others. People who compare themselves positively to others (they consider they are as able and as good as others) can be said to have a high self-esteem. Individuals who consider themselves to be less able and inferior to others have a low self-esteem. Our self-esteem has an impact on how we respond to other people. The way we and others perceive us and the value we have for ourselves have a great impact on our well-being.

Self-image is a mental picture we have of ourselves and it combines with self-esteem to form our identity. Our self-image develops through our relationships and interactions with others and this helps us to become aware of our physical, emotional, intellectual and social abilities, attributes and qualities.

  ACTIVITY

Read the statements below about people's sense of identity and self-esteem and explain how these thoughts and feelings would affect their sense of well-being.

1. My family have stopped coming to see me. I don't mean anything to them any more.

2. I've just had my first baby! I'm a mum now, more than a wife and daughter!

3. I've had my driving licence taken away as the government have decided I'm too old to drive. I'm just an old man who's a danger on the roads.

4. I've had to give up work because my multiple sclerosis has got so bad. I'm useless to any employer.

5. I've had a mastectomy but the implant is perfect!

6. I'm so fat. I just can't lose weight. It's all because of the medication.

  ACTIVITY

Think about two of the people you care for and support: one whose well-being is quite positive and another whose well-being is inclined to be negative. Why do they feel like this? Answer in terms of their self-esteem and sense of identity.

Person 1:

Person 2:

# Attitudes and approaches that are likely to promote well-being

You can help people whose well-being has been reduced by having a positive attitude and using approaches that help them rebuild their sense of peace and contentment.

  **ACTIVITY**

See how many words describing attitudes and approaches that are likely to promote well-being you can find in this wordsearch.

| | | | | | | | | | | | | | | | | |
|---|---|---|---|---|---|---|---|---|---|---|---|---|---|---|---|---|
| J | T | I | M | E | K | R | A | S | B | Z | I | K | U | Y | E | P |
| V | S | S | S | H | V | L | H | Q | Z | J | Q | T | K | G | U | P |
| T | T | O | A | D | M | I | R | E | E | U | C | Q | A | S | T | A |
| N | P | N | C | J | A | K | J | P | L | E | I | R | L | P | C | P |
| L | Y | R | X | I | T | S | L | Y | P | F | U | X | Q | A | O | L |
| Q | G | M | O | O | A | E | S | S | R | O | P | J | A | R | N | Z |
| F | W | Q | C | F | H | B | E | I | C | W | Y | G | D | T | G | U |
| V | T | F | X | L | E | R | L | N | S | K | C | C | V | N | R | C |
| E | D | K | R | I | G | S | E | E | P | T | W | X | O | E | A | P |
| J | R | E | M | I | N | I | S | C | E | N | C | E | C | R | T | A |
| A | E | T | E | X | E | E | B | I | M | G | S | H | A | S | U | T |
| D | C | O | M | P | A | N | Y | C | O | V | G | K | C | H | L | I |
| V | Z | T | W | P | R | N | D | V | Z | N | A | V | Y | I | A | E |
| I | P | R | A | I | S | E | K | L | Y | Z | A | M | B | P | T | N |
| C | C | N | U | U | D | Y | Q | Y | Y | P | T | L | Q | F | E | C |
| E | O | O | C | S | U | P | P | O | R | T | I | V | E | C | H | E |
| Q | C | A | R | I | N | G | U | G | Q | N | K | W | O | T | D | P |

encourage  praise  admire  congratulate  friendly  sociable  professional
respect  caring  supportive  advice  advocacy  company  assist
help  time  patience  reminiscence  partnership

# Promoting a sense of identity and self-esteem

## CASE STUDY

Rod, aged 54, has just been diagnosed with Alzheimer's disease, which affects physical and mental abilities, emotions and behaviour. He is married and has a child living at home. He has a position of responsibility at work, plays bridge and enjoys cycling. He is also involved with the Scout Association, where he is a Scout Leader. Rod is devastated by the diagnosis.

You have been assigned to support Rod.

1. How do you think the diagnosis will have affected Rod's sense of:

✿ identity?

✿ self-esteem?

2. Give one way you could help promote his identity and one way you could help promote his self-esteem.

✿ Identity:

✿ Self-esteem:

 ## ACTIVITY

Keep a record for a week to show how you help people develop and maintain their sense of identity and self-esteem. Ask them to confirm your support by initialling your entries.

# Promote well-being in the environment

Think about the environment you live in. If you have any say in the matter, it's probably very good for your well-being. For example, you probably have good, supportive relationships with the people you live with, but also space to be on your own, with your own thoughts, when you want. You're likely to be able to practise your religious and political beliefs and to keep up cultural customs and traditions. However, the people you care for and support may not live in an environment or with people of their choosing.

## ACTIVITY

Complete the table to show how you promote the well-being of one of the people you care for and support in the environment in which they live.

| Well-being | How I promote well-being in the environment where the person I care for and support lives |
|---|---|
| Spiritual. | |
| Emotional. | |
| Cultural. | |
| Religious. | |
| Social. | |
| Political. | |

# ARE YOU READY FOR ASSESSMENT?

☑ **Do you know the following:**

☐    1. The definition of person-centred values?

☐    2. The reasons for working in a person-centred way?

☐    3. The reason why risk can be part of a person-centred approach?

☐    4. How an individual's care plan contributes to working in a person-centred way?

☐    5. The importance of establishing consent when providing care and support?

☐    6. The action to take when consent is not easily established?

☐    7. How active participation benefits an individual?

☐    8. The possible barriers to active participation?

☐    9. The reasons why a worker's personal views should not influence an individual's choices?

☐    10. How to support an individual to question or challenge decisions concerning them that are made by others?

☐    11. How individual identity and self-esteem are linked with well-being?

☐    12. The attitudes and approaches that are likely to promote an individual's well-being?

☑ **Can you do the following?**

☐    1. Find out an individual's history, preferences, wishes and needs?

☐    2. Work in a person-centred way that takes into account an individual's history, preferences, wishes and needs?

☐    3. Establish consent when providing care and support?

☐    4. Encourage active participation and remove any potential or actual barriers to this?

☐    5. Support individuals to make informed choices?

☐    6. Use agreed risk assessment processes to support individuals' rights to make choices?

☐    7. Create an environment and work in ways that promote individuals' sense of identity, self-esteem and well-being?

# UNIT HSC 027

## Contribute to health and safety in health and social care

It's important that people who work in health and social care have a knowledge and understanding of health and safety legislation and how it affects the way they carry out their activities. It's also important that they develop the necessary skills to work safely and protect themselves and the people they care for and support from harm. This chapter gives you an opportunity to check your learning and understanding of health and safety and show that you work safely.

### You will need to be able to:

- ✿ understand your own and others' responsibilities relating to health and safety
- ✿ understand the use of risk assessments in relation to health and safety
- ✿ respond to accidents and sudden illness
- ✿ reduce the spread of infection
- ✿ move and handle objects and equipment safely
- ✿ safely handle hazardous substances and materials
- ✿ promote fire safety
- ✿ implement security measures
- ✿ manage stress.

# Health and safety responsibilities

## Health and safety legislation relating to where you work

Different activities are carried out in different work settings and there is a large amount of **health and safety legislation** to make sure these activities are carried out safely. It is important to remember to work within your job role. If you are unsure of the boundaries regarding your job role, then seek advice from your manager. Organisational policies and procedures will also guide you about your responsibilities, both legal and as an employee, as these will be based on health and safety legislation requirements.

### ACTIVITY

Make a list of five health and safety laws and regulations that are most relevant to your work setting. Talk to your manager, health and safety rep, assessor and colleagues; or you might consider looking at policies, procedures and induction files at work.

✿

✿

✿

✿

✿

## Health and safety policies and procedures where you work

Policies are based on laws and regulations, for example a manual handling policy is based on the Manual Handling Operations Regulations. Procedures describe the way activities have to be carried out so that policies are put into practice. For a manual handling policy to be put into practice, every manual handling activity will have to be carried out according to a set procedure.

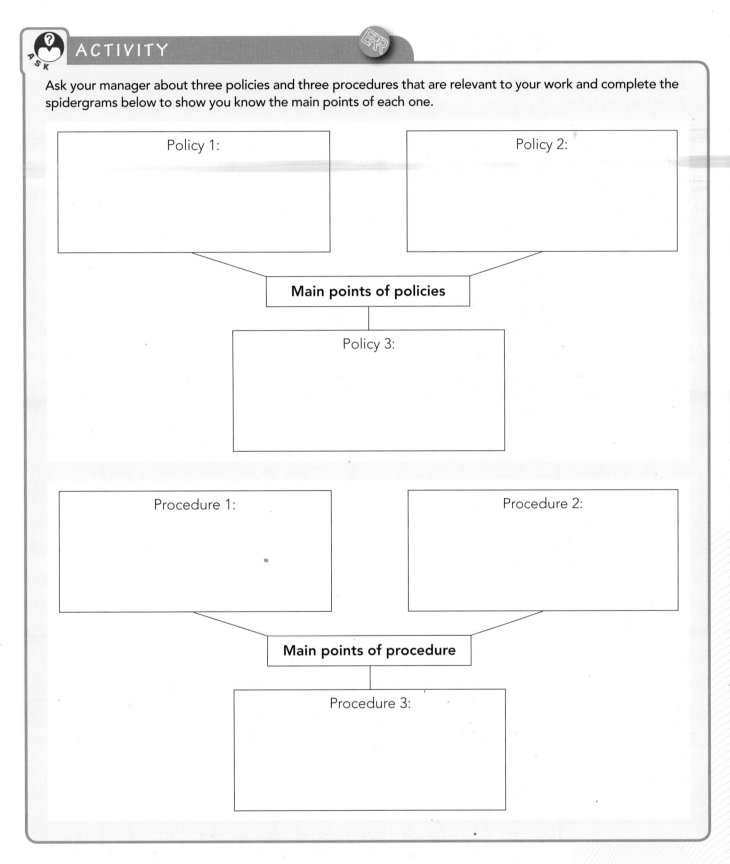

## ACTIVITY

Ask your manager about three policies and three procedures that are relevant to your work and complete the spidergrams below to show you know the main points of each one.

Policy 1:

Policy 2:

**Main points of policies**

Policy 3:

Procedure 1:

Procedure 2:

**Main points of procedure**

Procedure 3:

# Health and safety responsibilities where you work

Everyone at your work setting has a responsibility to protect themselves and others from harm. This includes your colleagues, the people you care for and support, and any visitors.

## ACTIVITY

Complete the gaps in the following sentences using the words below. Some words may be used more than once. This will show that you know the most important health and safety responsibilities for yourself and other employees.

> ability    care    change    cooperate    illnesses    injuries
> interfere    machinery    medication    misuse    policies    pregnant
> procedures    reasonable    training

The following are important health and safety responsibilities for people who work in health and social care settings.

✿ To take _____ care of their own health and safety.

✿ To take reasonable _____ not to put other people at risk by what they do or don't do in the course of their work.

✿ To _____ with their employer, making sure they get proper _____ and understand and follow their organisation's health and safety _____ and _____.

✿ Not to _____ with or _____ anything that's been provided for their health, safety or welfare.

✿ To report any _____ or _____ they get as a result of doing their job. Their employer may need to _____ the way they work.

✿ To tell their employer if something happens that might affect their _____ to work, for example becoming _____ or sustaining an injury.

✿ If they drive or operate _____, to tell their employer if they take _____ that makes them drowsy.

## ACTIVITY

Use an internet search engine to check out employers' health and safety responsibilities. List below the five that you think most apply to your employer and work setting. The websites www.direct.gov.uk and www.hse.gov.uk will give you lots of information.

✿

✿

✿

✿

✿

# Madge

**CASE STUDY**

Madge, aged 79, has moved into Holly Lodge, which is warden-assisted accommodation for older people. She has a small self-contained flat but there is a communal garden, lounge and laundry facility. Her family, including young grandchildren, visit regularly, as does the warden, her home cover and a volunteer befriender. Health and safety is taken very seriously at Holly Lodge and all residents and their visitors have a responsibility to protect themselves and others from harm.

List one health and safety responsibility for each of the following people involved in Madge's care.

✿ Madge:

✿ Madge's family:

✿ The warden:

✿ The home help:

✿ The volunteer befriender:

## Tasks related to health and safety

As you know, you have a responsibility to make sure you are properly trained to carry out your activities. Never carry out activities for which you haven't been trained or that you don't feel confident and **competent** to carry out safely.

**ACTIVITY**

Complete the spidergram with three activities for which you need special training. An example has been done for you.

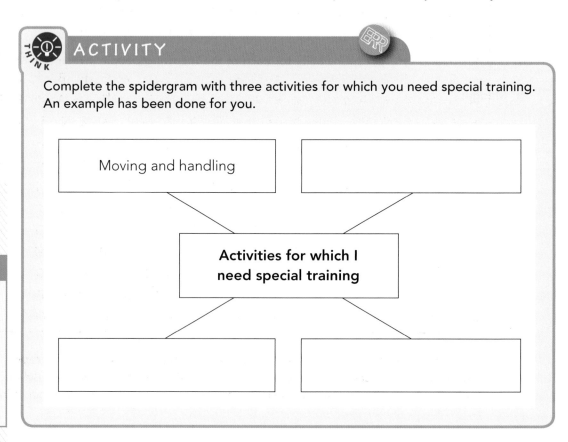

Moving and handling

Activities for which I need special training

**Assessor tip**

Procedure manuals in your work setting are a good source of information regarding health and safety legislation and responsibilities. Use these when gathering evidence for this unit.

# Accessing support and information about health and safety

There is no excuse for not knowing how to work safely.

 ACTIVITY

There are a great many sources of support and information about health and safety. See how many you can find in the wordsearch.

```
Y O L T X A R S A B N A B W L L D X L F E L J F L
G N K Q X M C A I J R J I U D L E A F L E T S I A
Y G P S U R G E R I E S T F X R W E B S I T E S O
M A N U F A C T U R E R S I N S T R U C T I O N S
H C B J T Y Z I N Y U K K C N Z Z L R L B V D G Z
E V I O E V H W F S C S H O S E T O M D H V K A F
A S A L N A O Z X S L M I D M M C R B K U O T P Y
L J O T G Q T S Z A F T R E A J E L Z Z T C I P Z
T T V E E T R Y N G A V B S N L I B R A R I E S Y
H H M X H M W R C T L Z J O A A L A G B I S N I N
A K I T V P U V S S P M O F G U Q W O J C W W K N
N S T B D O R E U E Y Q Z P E Q E J B B O P T P B
D B T O J K R O O K W I J R R A C L K L K M I V P
S B G O Z I Z Q C J Q G Q A S D W G R B J C X N O
A H M K F T L G M E X J J C N Y Z E U A W E N Q L
F C H S F F I W P L D H G T Z Q C X Z Z L Y D Y I
E C O L L E G E S T Y U L I S M L I X K F B X H C
T D S H M F U Z B U A L R C L G I B F L R G C P I
Y S P H Q R G U I D A N C E D O C U M E N T S C E
R I I D L M U J F Y F U W S K I W A C J Z Z Z S
E Y T Y S V D T A B E R L M Y M W T I J Q I H J D
P C A Z S P E U U V R E Z H Z B C M A B M S T X A
S I L T C O L L E A G U E S M D M W U T B Z H A I
S I S S G K E Y K T R A D E S U N I O N R E P S A
M P R F H E Y J H B U G Y L K O S C H O O L S I E
```

policies    procedures    websites    health and safety reps    trades union reps    libraries
colleagues    managers    hospitals    GP surgeries    fire stations    colleges    schools    journals
textbooks    leaflets    codes of practice    guidance documents    manufacturers instructions

# Health and safety risk assessments

## The importance of assessing health and safety hazards

A hazard is something that puts health and safety at risk. For example, faulty electrical equipment is a hazard – it poses a risk of fire. Before you carry out any activity or procedure, you must assess it for hazards so that you can control – reduce or eliminate – any associated risks. If you don't control risks, you expose everyone involved to possible harm.

## ACTIVITY

Complete the table to show that you understand five hazards at your work setting, the risks they pose and why it is important to assess the hazards. An example has been done for you.

| Hazard | Risk | Why I should assess hazards |
|---|---|---|
| Poor security. | Intruders. | To stop, or reduce, the risk of intruders and keep everyone safe. |
| | | |
| | | |
| | | |
| | | |
| | | |

## Reporting health and safety risks

You have a responsibility to report risks to health and safety as soon as you see them. This is so they can be dealt with straightaway and before they cause any harm. Your work setting should have an agreed procedure in place for reporting risks and hazards.

### ACTIVITY

Read the procedure your workplace has for reporting risks to health and safety. In your own words, in the space below, explain how and when you should report any risks that you identify.

Reporting risks

## Risk assessment and dilemmas between rights and health and safety concerns

Risk assessment is about identifying hazards and dealing with risks to protect people from harm. However, protecting people can deny them their right to take risks. If people you care for and support want to take risks, such as to stay independent even though they are frail, make them aware of the risks and be on the alert for a potential accident. In other words, manage the situation.

## Colin

### CASE STUDY

Colin, 65, is awaiting discharge from hospital after having a stroke that has left him partially paralysed and unable to speak clearly. The hospital wants him to go to a care home for a couple of weeks so that a physiotherapist, an occupational therapist and a social worker can assess his needs. The hospital thinks he will need all the help he can get to retain any quality of life. However, he insists on going home straightaway and being entirely independent. He says he has always 'done' for himself and nothing is going to stop him now. He doesn't want any help; he wants to be left to get on with his life as he chooses. He says he 'knows his rights'.

1. What concerns would you have for Colin's health and safety?

2. How could a risk assessment address his right to be independent and your concerns for his health and safety?

# Responding to accidents and sudden illness

Despite following health and safety procedures, accidents happen and people can become ill quite suddenly. You need to be able to respond to accidents and sudden illnesses. Look again at HSC 024, 'Principles of safeguarding and protection in health and social care' to remind yourself about the difference between signs and symptoms.

# Accidents and sudden illnesses where you work

Ask your colleagues to describe three accidents and three sudden illnesses that are most likely to occur at your work setting. Then complete the spidergram.

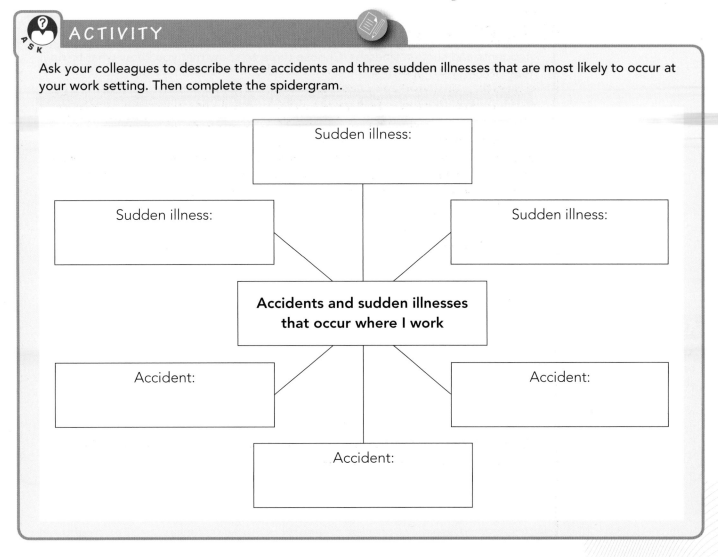

Sudden illness:

Sudden illness:

Sudden illness:

**Accidents and sudden illnesses that occur where I work**

Accident:

Accident:

Accident:

# Procedures to follow in the event of an accident or sudden illness

It's your responsibility to make sure you're trained in first aid and that your first aid training remains up-to-date.

Check your first aid certificate. Is it up-to-date? If not, ask your manager to book you onto a refresher course. If you aren't yet qualified in first aid, ask to go on a course as soon as possible.

## ACTIVITY

Build on the activity at the top of page 157, in which you identified common accidents and sudden illnesses. Choose three to show that you know what to do if they occur.

| Accident/sudden illness | What I should do if they occur |
|---|---|
|  |  |
|  |  |
|  |  |

**Assessor tip**

Attend a first aid course where you are able to practise first aid techniques. You will find it easier to explain what to do if you have actually experienced it or practised it.

# Reduce the spread of infection

You have a responsibility to reduce the likelihood of illness and infection by reducing the spread of bacteria and viruses. You can do this by:

* hand washing
* wearing personal protective clothing
* maintaining personal hygiene standards
* maintaining cleaning procedures and standards, for example dealing with laundry, disposing of waste appropriately
* dealing with spillages correctly and promptly
* notifying your employer if you have an infectious disease.

Look at ICO1/201 'The principles of infection prevention and control' to find out more about using personal protective clothing and infection control.

# Hand washing

## Your questions answered...

I get the feeling that hand washing is very important. I've just started working in a hospital and there are alcohol rub dispensers at the main entrance and the entrance to every ward; and there are posters in all the toilets and bathrooms telling you how to wash your hands properly. We even have volunteers whose role is to remind people to wash their hands before going onto the wards. Why is hand washing so important?

Quite rightly, your employer takes hand hygiene very seriously. Hand washing is one of the most important ways of controlling the spread of infections, especially infections that cause **respiratory disease** and diarrhoea and vomiting. Even when your hands look clean there is a risk that they carry infectious **microorganisms**, picked up during your normal day-to-day activities, which can put the health of vulnerable people, such as hospital inpatients, at risk. Washing your hands with soap and water, or with an alcohol rub, before having contact with people you care for and support, is the single most effective way of preventing the spread of infection.

**key terms**

**Respiratory diseases:** diseases of the lungs and body tissues that help us breathe.

**Microorganisms:** these include bacteria, fungi and viruses. They can only be seen through a microscope lens.

  ACTIVITY

Use an internet search engine to find out the recommended technique for washing your hands. You could try searching 'hand washing'. Use the space below to highlight some of the key steps in the correct hand washing technique.

Hand washing is important

  ACTIVITY

Ask your manager to observe you washing your hands. If you get it right, well done! If not, keep practising until you do.

# Personal health and hygiene

Many disease-causing microorganisms live on our bodies and in our clothes. As much of your work requires you to be physically close to vulnerable people, you need to have a good standard of personal hygiene and be healthy. Anything less encourages the spread of infection.

 **ACTIVITY**

In this wordsearch, see how many words you can find that relate to areas that require personal care and grooming.

```
R  K  C  W  O  U  N  D  S  D  J  F  U  A  J  E  D  U  P  P
W  H  R  B  N  D  C  I  O  F  P  O  N  N  A  F  K  R  S  Q
B  N  O  S  E  J  B  P  A  D  O  O  D  U  L  D  Z  M  V  S
C  P  C  D  K  M  S  S  V  Z  G  V  E  S  W  P  U  B  P  H
H  N  T  L  B  H  L  P  C  H  A  I  R  E  V  G  N  I  D  O
N  Q  F  M  O  A  J  Z  Z  G  W  C  A  G  L  H  L  L  A  E
A  P  R  K  T  T  T  E  E  T  H  Z  R  J  F  V  I  I  C  S
I  A  H  I  W  M  H  N  U  B  C  Y  M  C  O  D  B  I  F  Z
V  Y  N  G  J  I  V  E  I  H  E  Y  S  A  Q  R  F  X  J  T
F  E  J  F  S  K  I  N  S  Z  S  Q  U  F  E  H  X  S  X  B
G  M  W  E  X  P  W  R  D  D  N  O  B  G  P  P  I  O  M  C
M  H  I  E  N  L  B  H  N  F  W  Q  V  P  W  N  A  I  L  S
Q  O  E  A  R  S  A  A  P  J  L  N  G  B  M  X  M  W  Y  I
A  L  G  E  S  F  H  A  B  R  E  A  T  H  D  Y  B  A  Z  U
Y  Q  I  I  C  P  W  L  C  T  E  D  H  F  E  E  T  O  D  O
```

hair   skin   ears   nose   teeth   gums   breath   nails   hands
feet   underarms   genitals   anus   clothes   shoes   wounds

 **ACTIVITY**

Ask your manager what ill-health conditions should stop you going to work. List them below.

## Assessor tip

Remember, you can gather evidence of your competence in reducing the spread of infection whenever your assessor observes you undertaking a range of everyday work activities.

# Move and handle objects and equipment safely

About one in three injuries at work are caused by unsafe moving and handling, such as carrying, pushing, lifting and lowering. Moving and handling legislation is in place to protect you and the people you care for and support.

## Moving and handling legislation

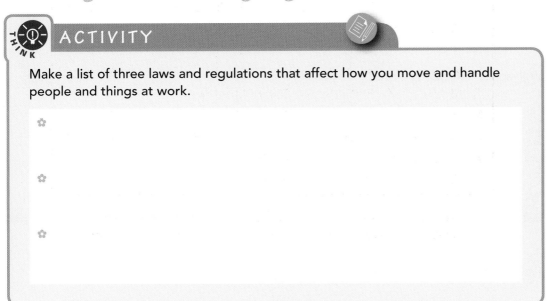

### ACTIVITY

Make a list of three laws and regulations that affect how you move and handle people and things at work.

✿

✿

✿

## The principles of safe moving and handling

There are a number of principles or rules that describe how to move and handle people and equipment safely.

 ACTIVITY

Complete the table to show that you understand why moving and handling must follow safe guidelines. The first one has been done for you.

| Safety guidelines | Reason for the guidelines |
|---|---|
| Avoid moving and handling wherever possible. | This eliminates all risk of injury. |
| Use equipment wherever possible. | |
| Don't carry out moving or handling activities unless you've been trained. | |
| Always follow procedures and risk assessments. | |
| Make sure there's enough space and that you can move comfortably. | |
| Use your large leg and buttock muscles to power you, and keep your back relaxed and in its natural S-shaped curve.<br>Bend at the knee, don't stoop or twist and, if you're holding the load, get a good grip and keep it close to your body. | |
| If you're helping a person to move, encourage them to help themselves. | |
| If you're working with colleagues, plan the move together and only have one person giving the orders, for example "1, 2, 3 move". | |
| Take your time and don't exceed your capabilities. | |

**ACTIVITY**

Complete the table to show that you understand both employer and employee responsibilities in relation to moving and handling by placing a tick in the correct column. The first one has been done for you.

| Responsibility for manual handling | Employer | Employee |
|---|---|---|
| Produce and implement a manual handling policy. | ✓ | |
| Provide induction and training courses. | | |
| Report any manual handling concerns. | | |
| Make sure individuals are fit to work. | | |
| Carry out risk assessments. | | |
| Monitor manual handling practice and seek advice from experts. | | |
| Be accountable for own actions. | | |
| Use all equipment appropriately and responsibly. | | |
| Provide equipment that is appropriate and in working order. | | |
| Investigate any injuries and aim to prevent reoccurrence through risk assessment. | | |

## Move and handle people and equipment safely

  **ACTIVITY**

Keep a record of how you contribute to safe moving and handling activities. Ask your manager to observe you at work and to confirm that you do indeed handle people and equipment safely.

The importance of posture

# Safe handling of hazardous substances and materials

## Hazardous substances and materials where you work

Hazardous substances and materials include cleaning materials, body fluids and waste, clinical waste, sharps and soiled linen. They are hazardous because they have the potential to affect health and safety.

**Assessor tip**

Remember that moving and handling doesn't just apply to working with individuals and using equipment. You can demonstrate the principles and your competence by moving and handling any load safely.

## ACTIVITY

Make a list of three hazardous substances and materials at your work setting and suggest how they can affect health and safety. An example has been done for you.

✿ Sharps, for example needles and scalpel blades. They can cause puncture wounds and spread infection.

✿

✿

✿

## ACTIVITY

Use an internet search engine to find out about employers' responsibilities under the Control of Substances Hazardous to Health (COSHH) Regulations (2002). Identify at least six responsibilities.

✿

✿

✿

✿

✿

✿

# Safe practices for storing, using and disposal of hazardous substances and materials

The Control of Substances Hazardous to Health (COSHH) Regulations require your employer to assess the risks from hazardous substances and materials and to write procedures that tell you how to store, use and dispose of them safely. In addition, manufacturers' instructions describe how to store, use and dispose of their products. It is your responsibility to know and follow these procedures and instructions precisely.

## ACTIVITY

Look back at the three hazardous substances and materials found at your work setting that you identified on page 164. Check your organisation's procedures and the manufacturers' instructions for their safe storage, use and disposal. Are you confident that you follow procedures and instructions correctly? Think about what could happen if you didn't.

## Caz

## CASE STUDY

Caz has just started working as a domestic at Safe As Houses residential care home for adults with learning difficulties. She enjoys the company of one of the residents, Jemima, so much that she invites her into the kitchen to chat, have a cup of tea, help with the washing up and so on. Jemima particularly loves to spring clean the cupboards, but she rearranges the various containers of cleaning materials, putting them where they don't belong. Caz also lets Jemima help her load the washing machine. Jemima loves the smell and feel of the liquid detergents and fabric conditioners, although she says they don't taste very nice! Caz also lets Jemima bag up the soiled linen. She likes to test her memory about which colour bag to put it in!

1. Caz isn't following safe practices. For a start, she shouldn't allow residents into the kitchen; but what should she do about:

 ✿ storing hazardous substances and materials, such as bleach and oven cleaner?

 ✿ using hazardous substances and materials, such as detergent and fabric conditioner?

✿ disposing of hazardous substances and materials, such as soiled linen?

2. What could happen as a result of her unsafe practices?

**Assessor tip**

You could describe safe practice for storing, using and disposing of hazardous substances while undertaking each task.

# Fire safety

Your organisation will have fire safety procedures and it is your responsibility to follow these precisely. It is also your responsibility to make sure that you are trained in fire safety and that your training remains up-to-date.

## Preventing fires from starting and spreading

  **ACTIVITY**

Complete the gaps in the following sentences using the words below. This will show that you know how to prevent a fire from starting and spreading.

blanket    contained    exclude    extinguisher    flammable    fuel
get    heat    out    oxygen    remove    safely    stored

**key term**

**Flammable:** inflammable, burnable.

For a fire to start, it needs:

✿ _____, that is, anything that is **flammable**

✿ _____, for example, a draught from an open door or window

✿ _____, for example, a lit cigarette or a spark from faulty electrical equipment.

To prevent a fire starting, make sure that anything that can catch fire is _____ _____ and away from a source of oxygen and heat.

To stop a fire from spreading:

✿ _____ anything nearby, that is _____ but don't put yourself in danger.

✿ _____ oxygen by closing all doors and windows.

✿ if it is small and _____, for example, in a chip pan or a bin, exclude the heat by smothering with a fire _____ or using a fire _____. There are different fire extinguishers for different types of fire, so make sure you use the right one.

✿ If the fire is spreading beyond your control, activate the fire alarm and _____ _____!

## Emergency procedures in the event of a fire

 ACTIVITY

Imagine that you're a care worker in a residential home for older people. Most of the residents are able-bodied, some have varying degrees of memory loss and challenging behaviour and a few choose to spend most of their time in their rooms. What would you do in the following emergency situations?

1. You discover a fire in the kitchen. It has taken hold and is too big for you to tackle.

2. You are with the residents in the lounge and the fire alarm goes off.

## Evacuation routes

Imagine trying to escape from a fire along a corridor that is dark and cluttered, with doors that don't open easily or are jammed shut, and with no sense of where to go. Now imagine that scenario for someone in a wheelchair, with learning difficulties or with a visual impairment.

Make sure you know the fire evacuation routes in your workplace

  **ACTIVITY**

Carry out a survey of fire evacuation routes in your workplace. Look for three barriers to evacuation, that is, things that could make evacuation difficult, such as obstructions, narrow corridors, a lack of grab rails or fire escape signs, and poor lighting. Complete the table to explain the importance of maintaining clear evacuation routes at all times. An example has been done for you.

| Barriers to evacuation | Why it is important to remove these barriers |
|---|---|
| Equipment blocking the corridor. | Equipment blocking corridors can cause accidents, for example, people falling over, which in turn causes other accidents, slowing people down and increasing risks to health and safety. |
| | |
| | |
| | |

**Assessor tip**

Your assessor could assess your knowledge and understanding during a walk through your workplace. As you escort them round the building, show them fire safety equipment, describe fire procedures and explain the reasons for keeping evacuation routes clear.

# Security measures

## Checking the identity of people who want access to your workplace or who ask for information

Your organisation will have procedures or agreed ways of working for checking the identity (ID) of anyone requesting access to your workplace or asking for information. You have a responsibility to follow these ways of working precisely so that people are not denied their right to be protected from harm and to have their personal information kept private.

## ACTIVITY

1. How do you check the ID of someone who requests entry to your workplace?

STAFF

Bob Smith
Notown Social Services
Dept
01234 567890

Checking ID

2. How do you check the ID of someone who phones your workplace requesting information about a colleague or someone you care for and support?

## ACTIVITY

Keep a record in which you describe how you check the ID of people requesting access to your workplace or information about colleagues and the people you care for and support. Ask your manager to observe you checking their ID and to confirm that you do indeed follow procedures and agreed ways of working.

## Protecting security at work

Your organisation should have a number of security measures in place to protect everyone where you work. You have a responsibility to cooperate with your employer in the use of these measures and to use them correctly. Not cooperating would deny people their right to be protected from harm.

**ACTIVITY**

Ask your manager about security measures at your workplace and how you are expected to use them. Complete the spidergram to show you know what could happen if you failed to use them properly. An example has been done for you.

Keep keypad codes secret. If I don't, unauthorised people could access the building and put safety at risk

**Security measures and why they must be implemented**

## The importance of letting people know where you are working

Your organisation should have procedures that enable workers to be located when they are out and about, for example when they are visiting patients at home and collecting and delivering prescriptions. These procedures are in place to protect workers, so they must be followed exactly.

  **ACTIVITY**

Use an internet search engine to find the 'We care because you care' domiciliary care lone worker safety guide, published by Skills for Care, 2010. Page 18 describes the procedures that employers should have in place to make sure they can protect the safety of workers who are out working on their own.

Use the guide to make notes about what workers need to tell their employers so that they can be traced at all times.

# Managing stress

In small measure, stress can be energising and motivating. However, too much can have a bad effect on our health and well-being. In fact, stress is a major cause of lost working days.

## Common signs and indicators of stress

Stress affects us physically, emotionally and intellectually, and causes changes to our behaviour.

 ACTIVITY

Complete the gaps in the following sentences using the words below. This will show that you know the common signs and indicators of stress.

anxiety   confidence   drug   heartbeat   memory   over-eating
attacks   concentration   sleep   sweating   tension   worrying

✿ The physical effects of stress include headaches, rapid _____,

muscle _____ and _____.

✿ The emotional effects of stress include panic _____,

_____, irritability and loss of _____.

✿ The intellectual effects of stress include _____ loss, poor

_____ and constant _____.

✿ Changes in behaviour due to stress include _____ loss,

_____ - _____, and alcohol and _____ abuse.

# Circumstances that trigger your stress

You need to know exactly what triggers your stress. Once you know that, you can work on managing your stress so that your health and well-being are not affected.

## ACTIVITY

Think about three activities that make you feel stressed, for example updating care plans. Now analyse each activity to help you identify exactly what it is that makes you feel stressed. For example, if updating care plans stresses you, is it because:

* you have to rush? Lack of time is a common **stressor**.
* so much depends on what you write in the care plan? Having responsibility can be stressful.
* you find it difficult to put your thoughts into writing? Many people find writing things down stressful.

| Activity | Stressor |
|---|---|
|  |  |
|  |  |
|  |  |

# Managing your stress

There are lots of ways of dealing with stress and different people have different coping strategies. What works for one person won't necessarily work for another.

 ACTIVITY

Think back to the three stressful activities you analysed in the previous activity. Use an internet search engine to explore different coping strategies and use your findings to describe how you can manage your stress. The NHS website is very informative – try www.nhs.uk/Livewell/Stressmanagement. An example has been done for you.

| Stressor | Coping strategy |
|---|---|
| Lack of time. | I need to plan my activities so I have time to do them without rushing. If anyone asks me to do a job that means I'll have to rush, I must tell them that I don't have time. I mustn't say 'yes' to a request if it puts my health and well-being at risk. |
| | |
| | |
| | |

It is important to find someone at work who you feel able to talk to and who will help you manage any work-related stress, as you may be in breach of confidentiality to discuss work matters outside the workplace. Stress related to work can only be resolved through things changing at work, and this can only occur if advice and support are sought through your employer. Your employer may provide a confidential service to provide advice and support.

# ARE YOU READY FOR ASSESSMENT?

☑ **Do you know the following:**

☐ **1.** The main points of the general health and safety legislation that applies to health and social care settings?

☐ **2.** The main responsibilities that you, your employer and others in the work setting have in relation to health and safety?

☐ **3.** The work tasks that require special training before you can carry them out?

☐ **4.** How to access additional support and information in relation to health and safety?

☐ **5.** The reasons why health and safety hazards related to either the work setting or activities must be assessed?

☐ **6.** How and when to report potential health and safety risks?

☐ **7.** How risk assessments can address the dilemmas between rights and health and safety concerns?

☐ **8.** The different types of accidents and sudden illnesses than can happen in your work setting and what to do if they occur?

☐ **9.** The legislation and principles that apply to moving and handling equipment and objects safely?

☐ **10.** The hazardous substances and materials found in your work setting and how to store, use and dispose of them safely?

☐ **11.** How to prevent fires starting and spreading?

☐ **12.** The procedures to follow in the event of a fire, to keep evacuation routes clear and for safe evacuation in an emergency?

☐ **13.** The reasons for ensuring others know your whereabouts while you are in the workplace?

☐ **14.** The common signs of stress?

☐ **15.** Your own stress triggers and how to manage these?

☑ **Can you do the following?**

☐ **1.** Wash your hands according to the recommended procedure?

☐ **2.** Ensure your own health and hygiene standards at work do not pose a risk to others?

☐ **3.** Check the identity of anyone wishing to access your workplace or information?

☐ **4.** Take appropriate action to ensure you and others in your workplace are safe and secure?

# UNIT HSC 028

## Handle information in health and social care settings

Unless information about people using health and social care services is recorded, stored and shared correctly, their needs will not be met. In addition, they have a right for personal and sensitive information about them to be kept private, that is, confidential. You have a responsibility to make sure that you handle information according to agreed ways of working and to maintain its confidentiality.

This chapter gives you an opportunity to show that you can handle information in ways that are agreed with your employer and that you promote the right to confidentiality of the people you care for and support.

**You will need to be able to:**
* understand the need for secure handling of information in your work setting
* know how to access support for handling information
* handle information according to agreed ways of working

# Secure handling of information in your work setting

## Legislation that relates to recording, storage and sharing of information in health and social care

Information in health and social care is recorded, stored and shared in a great many ways.

### ACTIVITY

Complete the crossword to show that you know some of the different ways that information is recorded, handled and shared in health and social care settings.

**Across**

4. Paper record shared by post. (6)
5. Electronic storage device in a computer. (4, 5)
6. Electronic record, usually of numbers. (11)
9. Written agreement about how a service user's health is managed, used in social care settings. (4, 4)
10. A record or message that can be sent electronically. (5)
11. Written record used in health care settings. (6, 6)
12. Portable electronic storage device. (6, 5)

**Down**

1. Electronic storage folder. (4)
2. Electronic record, usually of words. (4, 8)
3. Imaging record used in health care settings. (4)
7. Paper record used in schools. (8)
8. Paper record of a meeting. (7)

There are various laws and regulations that aim to protect information, to keep it confidential and to prevent it from going somewhere where it isn't authorised to go.

## ACTIVITY

Use the space below to list three laws and regulations relating to recording, storing and sharing of information in health and social care that are important to your work setting.

✿

✿

✿

Laws can protect information

## ACTIVITY

Search the internet for 'The Caldicott Principles' and then complete the gaps in the following sentences by selecting the correct word from the list below.

share   minimum   necessary   justify   law
understand   access   strict   responsibilities

People using personal information:

✿ must be able to _____ the purpose of every proposed use or transfer of information

✿ should not use or _____ personal information unless it is absolutely _____

✿ should use the _____ amount of personal information necessary to do a particular task.

In addition:

✿ _____ to personal information should be on a _____ need-to-know basis

✿ everyone with access to personal information must be aware of their _____

✿ everyone must _____ and comply with the _____.

Look again at SHC21 'Introduction to communication in health and social care settings' on page 12 to remind you about the principles of the Data Protection Act (1998) and other pieces of legislation.

## Secure systems for recording and storing information in health and social care settings

To care for and support people **holistically**, you need to know a great deal about them. Much of the information they give you will be quite personal and sensitive.

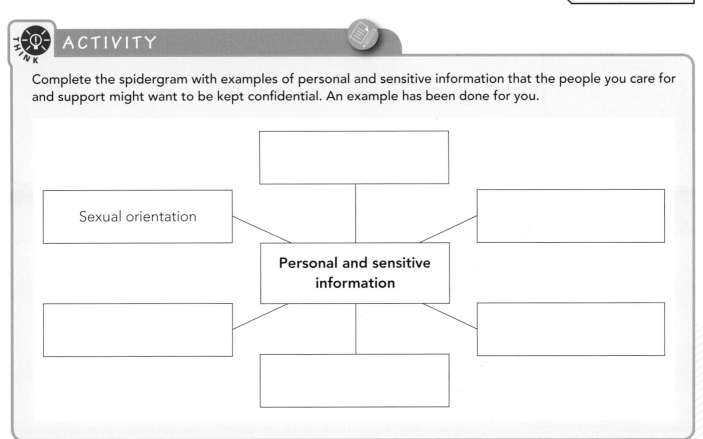

**ACTIVITY**

Complete the spidergram with examples of personal and sensitive information that the people you care for and support might want to be kept confidential. An example has been done for you.

Sexual orientation

**Personal and sensitive information**

Secure systems are the structures and ways of working that are used for maintaining confidentiality when you record and store information.

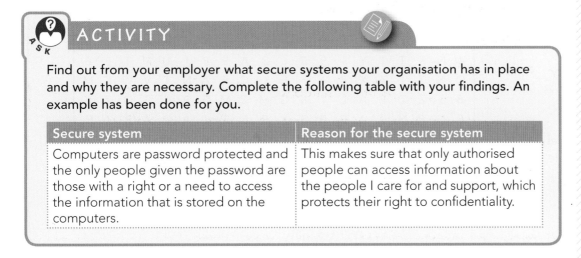

**ACTIVITY**

Find out from your employer what secure systems your organisation has in place and why they are necessary. Complete the following table with your findings. An example has been done for you.

| Secure system | Reason for the secure system |
|---|---|
| Computers are password protected and the only people given the password are those with a right or a need to access the information that is stored on the computers. | This makes sure that only authorised people can access information about the people I care for and support, which protects their right to confidentiality. |

| Secure system | Reason for the secure system |
|---|---|
| | |
| | |
| | |

## Assessor tip

As you show your assessor where service user records are kept, explain how you keep information secure when recording, storing and handling it, and the legal and organisational reasons for this.

## ACTIVITY

See how many secure systems and ways of working for recording and storing information in health and social care settings you can find in this wordsearch.

restricted access
locks
keys
privacy screen
virus protection
password
username
encryption
keypad
named key holder
policies
procedures
privacy
anonymity
discreet
careful
caution
confidential
responsible
trustworthy

```
P C O N F I D E N T I A L H C C G V I V
A N A M E D K E Y H O L D E R U K E Y S
S F D A F A W X D B T R Z G I L G S L S
S E I P L N J H R A G E S O T S E O V E
W D S H P O Z R E H R S U P P R G O I P
O K C D O N R T T E V T V M U I W V R R
R S R E L Y E E P H Q R V D A P H D U I
D Y E N I M S X U E B I E Y T V M B S V
G L E C C I P I L H Y C Y P F J I T P A
T M T R I T O Z W K O T L K I L N R R C
C U L Y E Y N S Z R Y E R E S C D U O Y
J P F P S T S M P M H D F Y A A L S T V
W N K T I Y I S R L Z A R P I U M T E B
O X Z I A X B A P E L C E A N T V W C M
B I Z O F A L T K G M C M D B I S O T C
E N R N J A E B S X R E T J A O A R I H
M L O C K S R J W L T S U J V N V T O W
C A R E F U L S E A J S Y Y E L U H N I
P R I V A C Y S C R E E N E A F T Y Z X
A X M T H Y U S E R N A M E X G A D B T
```

# How to access support for handling information

## Accessing guidance, information and advice about handling information

### ACTIVITY

Complete the gaps in the following sentences using the words below. This will show that you understand when health and social care workers might need guidance, information and advice about handling information.

confidential   give   memory   name   password
recognise   sign   stick   voice

✿ A visitor you don't _____ asks for information about someone you support.

✿ Someone whose _____ or _____ you don't recognise telephones for information about a colleague or patient.

✿ A colleague asks you for your computer _____ so she can check a patient's records, but you've been told not to _____ it to anyone else.

✿ You back up electronic records about clients on a _____ _____. A colleague wants to borrow it over the weekend, to save some letters she wants to write.

✿ You have responsibility for ensuring that if anyone takes a _____ file from the office, they must _____ to say they have taken it. Someone who is more senior to you wants to borrow a file but says they don't have time to sign.

If you ever have any concerns about how to handle confidential information, you must seek help.

## Your questions answered...

I'm very worried. I'm new in my role as receptionist at a residential care home for older people. I've just had a phone call from someone asking about Mrs Martin, who has dementia and is very poorly. The person claims to be a relative, but according to Mrs Martin's care plan, the only family she has are in Australia and they've never written or been to visit since she's been here, which is about five years. I'm worried in case this person is just after her money. What should I do?

This is a difficult situation, but one that happens quite frequently. There are several things you can do. First and foremost, talk with Mrs Martin about the caller. Does she know this person? Would she mind you giving out her personal information? If she's unable to confirm who they are, tell them politely that you can't give any information until you've verified their ID. Your workplace should have a procedure for checking ID – make sure you follow it. If the person can't, or isn't prepared, to have an ID check, or you're not confident about who the person really is, ask your manager to handle the call. Remember, all information held about the people you care for and support must stay confidential unless they or your manager gives you permission to share it.

Your workplace should have a procedure for checking ID

 **ACTIVITY**

Complete the spidergram with people and organisations that you can go to for guidance, information and advice about handling information. The first one has been done for you.

| My manager | |
|---|---|

**Sources of guidance, information and advice about handling information**

# What to do when there are concerns over the recording, storing or sharing of information

If you're ever concerned about the way that information is handled, especially when confidentiality is being **breached**, get help. Doing nothing is not an option. Denying people their right to privacy and confidentiality results in a lack of dignity, respect and best practice.

 ACTIVITY

Think about the following situations and identify the potential areas for concern regarding the recording, storing and handling of information, and what action can be taken to reduce the risk of breaching confidentiality.

1. A domiciliary care worker keeping their work diary in their car.

   Potential concern:

   Action to reduce risk:

2. Working from home.

   Potential concern:

   Action to reduce risk:

3. Travelling on public transport between service user visits in the community.

   Potential concern:

Action to reduce risk:

4. Sharing an office with workers from other agencies.

Potential concern:

Action to reduce risk:

# Breach of confidentiality

 **CASE STUDY**

Read the following scenarios and answer the questions to show that you understand how a breach of confidentiality can affect people.

Lucy accompanies a young man whom she supports to an outpatient appointment. The waiting room is very crowded and the receptionist doesn't take care to speak **discreetly** with everyone who reports to her desk. As a result, Lucy, and all the other people in the waiting room, get to hear the personal details of everyone attending. In addition, she answers the phone while registering the young man Lucy is with, asking the caller to wait on the phone while she finishes with him.

1. What is the problem here?

Breaching confidentiality

2. How might this situation impact on the patients in the waiting room, including the young man?

Mike is using a computer to update someone's care plan. The patient **self-administers** their medication and has taken an overdose. A cleaner with whom Mike is friendly comes and sits with him and reads what he is writing. She doesn't know the patient well but knows their family. She asks whether Mike has told the family about the overdose. She says that if Mike hasn't, she will.

3. What is the problem here?

4. How might this situation impact on the patient, their family and Mike?

## key term

**Self-administer:** to be responsible for taking your own medication.

## Assessor tip

Find out who is responsible for managing confidential information and data in your work setting and how to get access to them for advice and guidance.

 ACTIVITY

Complete the table below to show how you maintain confidentiality of information and what you would do if you were concerned that confidentiality was being breached. An example has been done for you.

| Examples of confidential information that you record, store or share | How do you ensure confidentiality? | What would you do if you were concerned that confidentiality was being breached? | Why would you take that action? |
|---|---|---|---|
| Paper copies of care plans. They are confidential because they contain personal and sensitive information about the people I support. | Care plans are kept in files, which are marked confidential, and when not in use they're stored in a locked filing cabinet. I have to ask the keyholder for access to the filing cabinet, sign and date a log to show when I take the file out of the cabinet and sign and date it again when I put the file back. | I would report my concerns to the keyholder and my manager. | I don't have the authority to check things out myself, nor do I have the seniority to challenge anyone. However, the keyholder should know who has had access to files and my manager is in a position to investigate. |
|  |  |  |  |
|  |  |  |  |
|  |  |  |  |

# Handle information according to agreed ways of working

## Keep records that are up-to-date, complete, accurate and legible

Records need to be written so that other people can understand and act on the information if necessary. If something isn't clear, or does not accurately reflect a situation, people reading it may not be able to provide the individual with good care and support, and it may even put the individual at risk of harm. This means you should report only what has been agreed or what has happened, rather than your own opinions.

Part of producing an accurate and legible record is to use correct grammar, spelling and punctuation. Try not to use jargon or abbreviations that other people might not understand. If your handwriting isn't very clear, type the report.

  ACTIVITY

1. **What do you think of the following entry in Dorothy's care plan?**

*"Dorothy was a pane this mourn. Shed a rate old moan at me wen I went t get her dressed. She's got another brooze on her faze. Appen shes fell ovva again. It's n wonder er family calls er Dotty."*

2. **In what way does the entry contradict the need for records to be:**

✿ up-to-date?

✿ complete?

✿ accurate?

Record keeping

✿ legible?

## ACTIVITY

Complete the gaps in the following sentences using the words below. This will show that you understand the importance of making records that are up-to-date, complete, accurate and legible.

clear  errors  incomplete  influence  information  mistakes
needs  opinions  understand  unimportant  up-to-date

Records you make must be:

✿ neat and _____, so that others can read and
_____ them easily

✿ correct, as _____ can lead to _____ in the way people are cared for and supported

✿ current, as records that are not _____-_____-_____ can lead to care and support that is inappropriate, no longer necessary or wrong

✿ full and comprehensive, as _____ records lead to care and support that fails to meet all of a person's _____

✿ objective and impartial, as records that express _____ and feelings can have a negative _____ on care and support

✿ relevant and concise, as records that ramble or include _____ _____ rely on people who are already busy having enough time and concentration to identify the important parts.

## ACTIVITY

Ask your manager to give you feedback on the way you handle information. Do you keep records that are up-to-date, complete, accurate and legible? If you do, well done! If you need to make improvements, where can you get help? Complete the following spidergram to show that you know where you can go for help in record keeping. An example has been done for you.

```
┌─────────────────────────┐              ┌─────────────────────────┐
│  An adult literacy course │              │                         │
│     at my local college   │              │                         │
└─────────────────────────┘              └─────────────────────────┘
              \                                      /
               \        ┌─────────────────────┐    /
                \       │ Sources of help and  │   /
                 \      │   advice on record   │  /
                 /      │      keeping          │  \
                /       └─────────────────────┘   \
               /                                    \
┌─────────────────────────┐              ┌─────────────────────────┐
│                         │              │                         │
└─────────────────────────┘              └─────────────────────────┘
```

## Follow agreed ways of working

You have a responsibility to make sure that you handle information according to agreed ways of working. Agreed ways of working include policies and procedures, and your workplace will have agreed ways of working for recording, storing and sharing information.

## ACTIVITY

Check out the information handling procedures for your workplace.

Complete the following table to show that you understand your roles and responsibilities when recording, storing and sharing information.

| Information handling | My roles and responsibilities |
|---|---|
| Recording information. | |

| Information handling | My roles and responsibilities |
| --- | --- |
| Storing information. | |
| Sharing information. | |

## ACTIVITY

Keep a record of how you handle information in line with agreed ways of working. Ask your manager to verify that you do follow agreed ways of working at all times by initialling your entries.

## ARE YOU READY FOR ASSESSMENT?

☑ **Do you know the following:**

☐ **1.** The main points of the legislation that apply to recording, storing and sharing information in health and social care settings?

☐ **2.** The reasons why secure systems for recording and storing information in a health and social care setting are so important?

☐ **3.** How to access guidance, information and advice about handling information?

☐ **4.** The actions to take when there are concerns about recording, storing or sharing information?

☑ **Can you do the following:**

☐ **1.** Keep up-to-date, complete, accurate and legible records?

☐ **2.** Record, store and share information according to agreed ways of working?

# UNIT DEM 201

## Dementia awareness

As we get older, we become more likely to develop degenerative diseases. A degenerative disease is one in which the body tissues and organs deteriorate over time. Dementia is a degenerative disease, and because the population of older people is growing, the **incidence of dementia could rise quite markedly**. To give people with dementia quality care and support, you need to be familiar with all aspects of the condition.

This chapter gives you an opportunity to show that you know and understand about dementia – including its causes, signs and symptoms – and how it affects people's lives.

**You will need to be able to:**
- ✿ understand what dementia is
- ✿ understand key features of the theoretical models of dementia
- ✿ know the most common types of dementia and their causes
- ✿ understand factors relating to an individual's experience of dementia.

# Understand what dementia is

## Explain the meaning of the term 'dementia'

  **ACTIVITY**

Use a dictionary or an internet search engine to find out what the term 'dementia' means. You could try searching the term 'define dementia'. Put what you find into your own words, making sure you don't lose any meaning.

Now check out three other people's definition of dementia and write their ideas below. How do their definitions compare with the correct one?

✿

✿

✿

From your research you will have found out that dementia is a long-term condition that mainly affects people over the age of 65, although some forms can affect people much younger than this. Dementia covers a range of symptoms, the combination of which depends on the specific type of dementia and parts of the brain affected.

# Functions of the brain that are affected by dementia

## ACTIVITY

Complete the table to show that you know what functions of the brain are affected by dementia. The first one has been done for you.

Note that www.alzheimers.org.uk, Factsheet 456 'The brain and behaviour' is very clear about loss of function as parts of the brain become diseased.

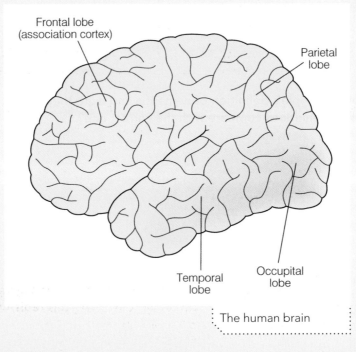

Frontal lobe (association cortex)

Parietal lobe

Temporal lobe

Occupital lobe

The human brain

| Parts of the brain that are affected by dementia | How damage to these areas affects the person who has dementia |
|---|---|
| The occipital lobe. | The person loses their ability to **perceive** colour, shape and movement. |
| The parietal lobe. | |
| The temporal lobe. | |
| The frontal lobe. | |
| The limbic system (deep in the centre of the brain). | |

# Depression, delirium, age-related memory loss and dementia

The symptoms of depression, delirium, age-related memory loss and dementia are very similar. However, the conditions are not the same and are treated differently. A wrong diagnosis means that the person concerned won't get appropriate care and support. A person with age-related memory impairment, while finding remembering things more difficult, will continue to recognise people, places and objects even though they may be unable to actually name them.

## ACTIVITY

1. Ask your manager or use an internet search engine to remind yourself of the signs and symptoms of depression, delirium and age-related memory loss. From your research complete the following sentence.

   The main difference between age-related memory loss and other forms of memory loss related to dementia is:

2. Complete the table by placing the symptoms in the correct columns. Some symptoms are shared, so these can be placed in more than one column. Correctly completing this table will show that you know the differences between dementia, depression and delirium.

Loss of ability to read and write
Rapid mental decline
Negative view of life
Short-term memory loss
Apathy
Problems with time

Unconsciousness
Inability to maintain concentration
Low motivation
Memory problems
Poor attention span
Slow mental decline

Slow movements
Increasing disorientation
Slow speech
Mental incoherence
Progressive confusion

| Dementia | Depression | Delirium |
|---|---|---|
|  |  |  |

## Maureen

 **CASE STUDY**

Maureen, aged 84, has had a urinary tract infection (UTI) for some time and has started to forget things, such as where she's put her keys and the procedures she uses at her weekly computer course for logging into accounts. She's also easily agitated and quarrelsome with the neighbours, and sometimes lacks awareness about what day it is and where she is, which makes her feel wretched and miserable. However, she knows that she has her good moments and that these bouts of sadness don't last long. When the gloom lifts, she's back to her usual good-natured self.

Her family thinks she may have dementia. Give three reasons why they might think this and explain why they could be wrong.

✿

✿

✿

## Models of dementia

### Medical and social models of dementia

The medical model of dementia promotes the idea that people with dementia are like broken machines and need to be 'managed' to stop them being a problem. The social model of dementia promotes the idea that it is society that is the problem, because society's attitudes and ways of doing things restrict the way people with dementia can live. It requires society to change so that no one's life is restricted because they are different.

## ACTIVITY

John has a form of dementia called dementia with Lewy bodies (DLB). He has muscle tremors (shaking), muscle rigidity (stiffness) and is losing his facial expression and ability to speak. This means it takes him a long time to do things, he is liable to fall and he has problems communicating. He is also very depressed, has memory problems and is easily **disorientated**.

Complete the table to show you know the differences between the medical and the social model of caring for someone with DLB. An example has been done for you.

| John's needs | How someone who uses the medical model would care for and support John | How someone who uses the social model might care for and support John |
|---|---|---|
| Mobility. | They might give him medication to help control the tremors and rigidity. | They might give him a wheelchair and make sure there are no barriers to prevent him going wherever he wants in the wheelchair. |
| Falls. | | |
| Communication. | | |
| Depression. | | |
| Impaired memory. | | |
| Disorientation. | | |

## Dementia as a disability

### ACTIVITY

Use an internet search engine to define the term 'disability' or look it up in a dictionary. Write the definition below.

Dementia puts people out of action. It disables them mentally and physically, taking away their independence and restricting their lives. As result, they are also disabled socially and emotionally.

### ACTIVITY

Think about someone you know who has been diagnosed as having dementia. Describe how the dementia affects them and explain why they are disabled as a result. An example has been done for you.

✿ The dementia means they have a problem remembering things, for example they forget arrangements to meet with friends and family. This is disabling because it means their ability to participate in social activities is being lost.

✿

✿

✿

# Common types of dementia and their causes

There are more than 100 different types of dementia, each with its own particular cause.

## Common causes of dementia

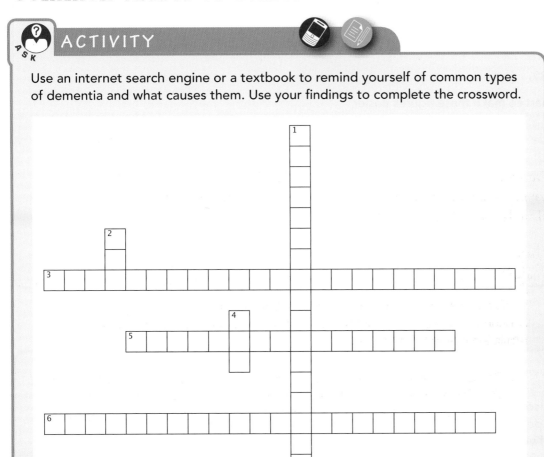

ACTIVITY

Use an internet search engine or a textbook to remind yourself of common types of dementia and what causes them. Use your findings to complete the crossword.

### Across

3. A condition used to describe people who have some problems with their memory (4, 9, 10)
5. A condition caused by blockages in blood vessels in the brain (8, 8)
6. A condition caused by damage to the front of the brain (6, 8, 8)

### Down

1. A disease caused by an accumulation of **plaques** and **tangles** in and around the brain cells (10, 7)
2. A condition caused by **prions** invading the brain (3)
4. A condition caused by the presence of **Lewy bodies** in the brain cells (3)

## ACTIVITY

According to the Alzheimer's Society, the proportions or percentages of people with the most common types of dementia can be broken down as follows:

- ✿ Alzheimer's disease (AD): 62%
- ✿ vascular dementia (VaD): 17%
- ✿ mixed dementia (AD and VaD): 10%
- ✿ dementia with Lewy bodies: 4%
- ✿ fronto-temporal dementia: 2%
- ✿ Parkinson's dementia: 2%
- ✿ other dementias: 3%

Draw a labelled bar chart to make these figures easier to understand.

## ACTIVITY

Ask your manager how many people at your work setting have dementia, and of those, how many have Alzheimer's disease, vascular dementia, and so on. If you don't work with people who have dementia, identify whether any of your friends and family have dementia and, of them, how many have one or other of the different types of dementia.

Convert the figures you collect into percentages and draw a labelled bar chart, headed either 'Proportions of people with different types of dementia in my work setting' or 'Proportions of people I know with different types of dementia.'

# Signs and symptoms of the most common causes of dementia

**ACTIVITY**

Here is a list of the signs and symptoms commonly associated with the four main types of dementia: Alzheimer's disease; dementia with Lewy bodies; vascular dementia, and fronto-temporal dementia. Complete the table by matching the correct signs and symptoms to the type of dementia. Don't forget some signs and symptoms may be common to more than one type of dementia.

| | | |
|---|---|---|
| Confusion | Poor mobility | Inattentive |
| **Perseveration** | Rituals | Aggression |
| Disinterest | Incontinence | Forgetful of recent events |
| Fainting and falling | Wandering | Unresponsive |
| Personality change | Mood swings | Inappropriate sexual behaviour |
| **Confabulation** | Non-empathetic | Loss of facial expression |
| Delusions | Disorientation | Decline in problem-solving skills |
| Indecision | Sleepy | Rapid shuffling steps |
| Memory loss | Loss of **faculty** | Lack of **insight** |
| Loss of inhibitions | Repetition | Gradual deterioration |
| Depression | Inappropriate behaviour | |
| Hallucinations | Restlessness | |
| | Poor communication | |

**key terms**

**Perseveration:** repetition of a particular word, phrase or gesture.
**Confabulation:** an unconscious filling in of the gaps in the memory that the person believes to be true.
**Faculty:** capability, such as mental capability.
**Insight:** the ability to see into a situation.

| Alzheimer's disease | Dementia with Lewy bodies | Vascular dementia | Fronto-temporal dementia |
|---|---|---|---|
| | | | |

## ACTIVITY

Think about two people you know who each have a different type of dementia. Complete the table to show that you are aware of the signs and symptoms of their type of dementia. An example has been done for you.

| Person and the type of dementia they have (remember confidentiality) | Signs and symptoms |
|---|---|
| Mrs A. She has DLB. | She has difficulty moving – she shuffles; and difficulty communicating with me – she can't use body language and it takes her a long time to say anything. She is quite sluggish and sleeps a lot. She doesn't sleep well: she has nightmares and wakes up very confused. She can't remember much, except what she did as a child. She has difficulty paying attention and thinking about things. |
|  |  |
|  |  |

## Risk factors for common types of dementia

Scientists have found several risk factors for dementia. While the risk factors don't cause dementia, they do increase our chances of developing the signs and symptoms.

## ACTIVITY

Complete the gaps in the following sentences using the words below. This will show that you know the risk factors for the common types of dementia.

cholesterol   diabetes   difficulties   greater   history   diet
learning   lifestyle   men   obese   older   women

Risk factors for common types of dementia include:

✿ age – the _____ we are, the _____ our chance of developing dementia

✿ gender – more _____ than _____ have dementia

✿ a family _____ of dementia

✿ health conditions such as high blood pressure, high _____, _____ and **atherosclerosis**

✿ _____ factors, such as eating an unhealthy _____, smoking, heavy drinking and lack of exercise

✿ being overweight or _____

✿ _____ _____, such as Down's syndrome.

Atherosclerosis

## Prevalence rates for different types of dementia

The **prevalence** of different types of dementia varies, according to, for example, age, sex and learning difficulty.

## ACTIVITY

Use an internet search engine to find out the up-to-date prevalence rates of different types of dementia within different groups of people. You could try searching for 'Prevalence rates for dementia'.

Write your findings below and, in your own words, summarise what the prevalence rates tell you.

### Assessor tip

Presenting your evidence using graphs, charts and diagrams may help you to remember the important facts.

## key terms

**Early onset dementia:** the term used for cases of dementia diagnosed before the age of 65.

# The experience of having dementia

## Living with dementia according to age, type of dementia, ability and disability

### CASE STUDY

Martin is 52. He is married with a son and grandchildren, aged 6 and 4. He is an accountant, plays golf, has a mortgage and a loan on his car. He has just been diagnosed with a rare form of **early onset dementia**. Complete the table to show you understand the impact of this diagnosis. Remember to consider the emotional physical, intellectual and financial impact, as well as the impact on daily living activities.

Note that the Alzheimer's Society website has a series of factsheets that you may find useful for doing this activity. See www.alzheimers.org.uk. On the internet you will also find personal stories from individuals with dementia, and their family and carers, which you may find useful when completing this activity. Remember that everyone's experience of dementia is unique.

Living with dementia

| People | Impact of the diagnosis |
|---|---|
| Martin. | |
| Martin's family. | |
| Martin's employer. | |
| Martin's friends. | |

## ACTIVITY

Complete the gaps in the following sentences using the words below. This will show that you know how having dementia can affect people with learning difficulties.

conversations   day-to-day   describe   questions
abilities   feelings   misunderstood   preferred   symptoms

Dementia is a loss of mental activity that affects:

✿ communication, for example, taking part in _____, answering _____ and describing feelings.

✿ behaviour, for example the ability to carry out _____-_____-_____ activities.

✿ There is no evidence that dementia affects people with learning difficulties differently from how it affects other people. However, the signs and _____ of dementia in someone with learning difficulties are more likely to be missed or _____. This is because they may find it hard to _____ how they feel and how their _____ have declined. In addition, problems with communication can make it difficult for others to assess change, particularly people who don't know them.

For these reasons, carers and care workers who support people with learning difficulties must:

✿ use the person's _____ method of communication at all times

✿ get to know and understand them so they can interpret their _____ and behaviour.

## Your questions answered...

My nan has just been diagnosed with Alzheimer's disease, which we know will affect her ability to remember, communicate, get about and understand. We want to make her life as comfortable as possible but don't know how we can help her. Can you please advise us?

How worrying for you all, but you are right to plan for the future. There are many ways to help people who are losing their abilities because of dementia. For example, as your nan's memory reduces, a dosette box (a pill organiser box) could prompt her to take her medication. If she starts to find it difficult to move about, she might find a walking frame useful. If she loses her ability to take part in social life and communicate her feelings, she may benefit from reminiscence therapy, which focuses on aspects of a person's life history that has brought them enjoyment and fulfilment. If she becomes confused and disorientated, for example about the date and time of day, an automatic clock and calendar could help. If she starts to wander, which can be very worrying, there are devices that enable you to record a voice prompt telling her, for example, to "Go back to bed – it's still night-time."

## ACTIVITY

There is a variety of equipment that can help with loss of ability brought about by having dementia. Complete the spidergram with examples of equipment that you think will help.

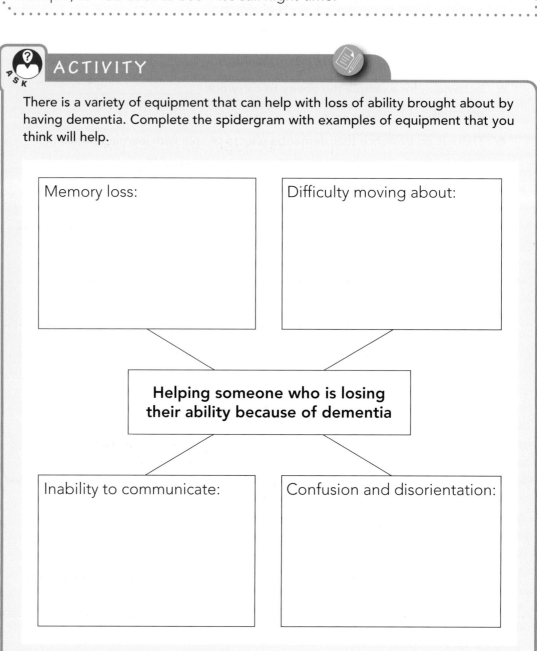

Memory loss:

Difficulty moving about:

**Helping someone who is losing their ability because of dementia**

Inability to communicate:

Confusion and disorientation:

**Assessor tip**

You could create an information sheet about dementia as evidence for your portfolio and that you could also share with colleagues and/or carers.

# The impact of other people's attitudes and behaviours

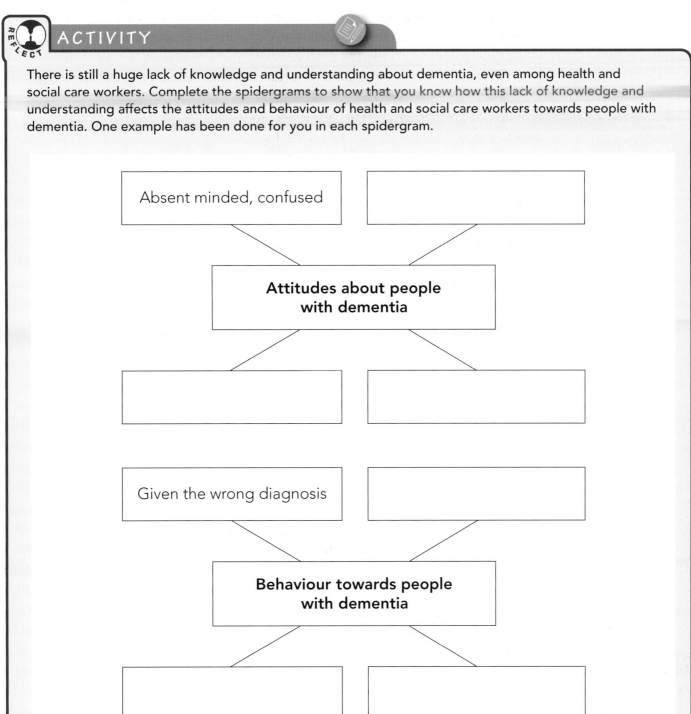

**ACTIVITY**

There is still a huge lack of knowledge and understanding about dementia, even among health and social care workers. Complete the spidergrams to show that you know how this lack of knowledge and understanding affects the attitudes and behaviour of health and social care workers towards people with dementia. One example has been done for you in each spidergram.

Absent minded, confused

**Attitudes about people with dementia**

Given the wrong diagnosis

**Behaviour towards people with dementia**

We all have a right to respect, to care and support that meets our needs and to freedom from discrimination. Being diagnosed with dementia is challenging enough without the burdens of negative attitudes and care and support that is based on ignorance.

## ACTIVITY

Here are some words that describe the impact that negative attitudes and inappropriate care and support have on people with dementia, their family and friends. Next to each one, write down the opposite, positive word. In the third column suggest how you can work with individuals to turn three of the negative attitudes into positives.

| Negative attitude and behaviour | Positive attitude and behaviour | How to change the negative to positive |
|---|---|---|
| Embarrassed | | |
| Ashamed | | |
| Disempowered | | |
| Stigmatised | | |
| Humiliated | | |
| Intimidated | | |
| Lonely | | |
| Isolated | | |
| Alone | | |
| Useless | | |
| Abnormal | | |
| Inadequate | | |
| Frightened | | |
| Unsupported | | |
| Destroyed | | |
| Worthless | | |
| Withdrawn | | |

# ARE YOU READY FOR ASSESSMENT?

☑ **Do you know the following:**

☐ **1.** The definition of dementia?

☐ **2.** The key functions of the bra.. ..fected by dementia?

☐ **3.** The reasons why depression, delirium and age-related memory impairment may be mistaken for dementia?

☐ **4** The medical and social models of disability?

☐ **5.** The reasons for viewing dementia as a disability?

☐ **6.** The most common causes of dementia, and the risk factors and prevalence rates for each?

☐ **7.** The likely signs and symptoms of different types of dementia?

☐ **8.** How different individuals experience dementia and the impact of diagnosis on their lives and of those people significant to them?

☐ **9.** The impact of the attitudes and behaviours of others on individuals with dementia?

# UNIT ICO1/201

## The principles of infection prevention and control

The people you care for and support may be ill or frail through disability or age. They may have unhealthy lifestyles or live in unhealthy conditions. Because of this, they're particularly vulnerable to infection. The principles of infection prevention and control are rules or standards that you must use in your work to reduce or eliminate the risk of spreading infectious diseases.

This chapter gives you an opportunity to show that you know and understand the principles of infection prevention and control and your roles and responsibilities in putting them into practice.

### You will need to be able to:

* understand roles and responsibilities in infection prevention and control
* understand legislation and policies relating to infection prevention and control
* understand systems and procedures relating to infection prevention and control
* understand the importance of risk assessment in relation to infection prevention and control
* understand the importance of personal protective equipment (PPE) in infection prevention and control
* understand the importance of good personal hygiene in infection prevention and control.

# Roles and responsibilities in infection prevention and control

## Your roles and responsibilities

As a health and social care worker you are responsible for being aware and responding appropriately to health and safety hazards and risks. Preventing the spread of infections that lead to ill health, such as bacteria or viruses, is a key responsibility for everyone involved in supporting individuals. An infection can spread rapidly when people are living and working close to one another and so it is essential that precautions are in place to prevent this happening. Many of the individuals supported in health and social care settings are physically vulnerable as they are already experiencing ill health, such as a heart condition or recovering from surgery. Poor health makes them more susceptible to infection and will delay their progress. Some infections such as Escherichia coli (E. coli), a bacteria associated with poor hygiene practices, can spread rapidly and can result in death. Preventing infection spread is very important if you are to keep individuals safe from harm. Employers and employees share the responsibility of infection prevention and control.

### ACTIVITY

An infection hazard is anything that puts people at risk of becoming infected. Complete the spidergram with examples of three **potential** infection hazards at your workplace. An example has been done for you.

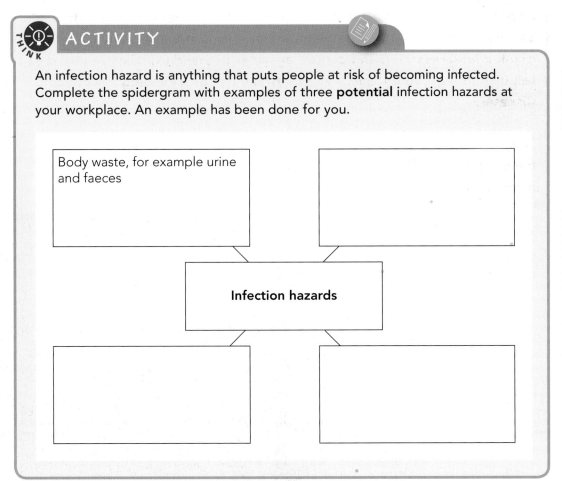

Body waste, for example urine and faeces

Infection hazards

### key term

**Potential:** possible, likely

ACTIVITY

Complete the following table to show you:

✿ know how to work to help prevent and control infection associated with the three hazards you identified in the activity on page 211

✿ know why you need to work in this way.

An example has been done for you.

| Hazard | What I have to do to help prevent and control the risk of infection | Why I need to work this way |
|---|---|---|
| Body waste, when someone has an accident in bed and soils the linen. | I have to follow procedures when dealing with soiled linen, for example I must wear personal protective equipment, take the linen in a red plastic bag to the laundry, and make sure the person concerned is clean and comfortable. I also have to report the accident to my manager. | The person who has the accident might have an infection, so these safety precautions help prevent the infection spreading. I need to tell my manager so that she can investigate whether the person has an infection or not. |
|  |  |  |
|  |  |  |
|  |  |  |

## Your employer's responsibilities

### ACTIVITY

Complete the gaps in the following sentences using the words below. This will show that you understand your employer's responsibilities about infection prevention and control.

immunised   notifiable   outbreaks   procedures
report   resistance   supervise   train

My employer has a responsibility to:

❀ write infection prevention and control _____ that tell me how I can help prevent and control infections

❀ _____ me in infection prevention and control procedures

❀ _____ me, to make sure I follow infection prevention and control procedures

❀ make sure I'm _____ against infectious diseases, so I'm not at risk of catching anything

❀ write an annual infection prevention and control _____, to tell people how our workplace deals with infection prevention and control and how it plans to improve its practices

❀ inform the local **Health Protection Unit** about suspected _____ of infection, _____ diseases and a change in _____ to antibiotics.

### key term

**Health Protection Units:** these deal with local public health issues. They are a part of the Health Protection Agency.

### Assessor tip

Ask your manager about attending an infection control course as this will provide you with the underpinning knowledge and understanding for this unit. If this is not possible, talk to the person who is responsible for infection control in your workplace.

# Legislation and policies relating to infection prevention and control

## Legislation and regulatory body standards relevant to infection prevention and control

There are a number of laws and regulations that aim to prevent and control infection, for example:

❀ Health and Safety at Work Act (HSWA).
❀ Management of Health and Safety at Work Regulations (MHSWR).
❀ Health and Social Care Act.
❀ Food Safety Act and Food Hygiene Regulations.
❀ Personal Protective Equipment Regulations.
❀ Control of Substances Hazardous to health Regulations (COSHH).

❀ Reporting of Injuries, Diseases and Dangerous Occurrences Regulations (RIDDOR).

❀ Hazardous Waste Regulations.

❀ Environmental Protection Regulations.

## CASE STUDY

Moving On is a new respite facility for young adults with mental health problems. The manager, Sheree, has to make sure that all her staff comply with legislation relating to infection prevention and control.

What laws and regulations relating to infection prevention and control specifically apply to the staff at Moving On?

❀ Chrissy, who is the cook.

❀ Derek, who is in charge of maintenance, cleaning, laundry and so on.

❀ Delia, who works in the office and deals with administration, paperwork and so on.

❀ Jane, who is a qualified nurse with responsibility for administering medication, monitoring health, and so on.

❀ Sheree.

## ACTIVITY

Complete the spidergram with three of your day-to-day work activities and the laws or regulations relating to infection prevention and control that govern how you carry them out.

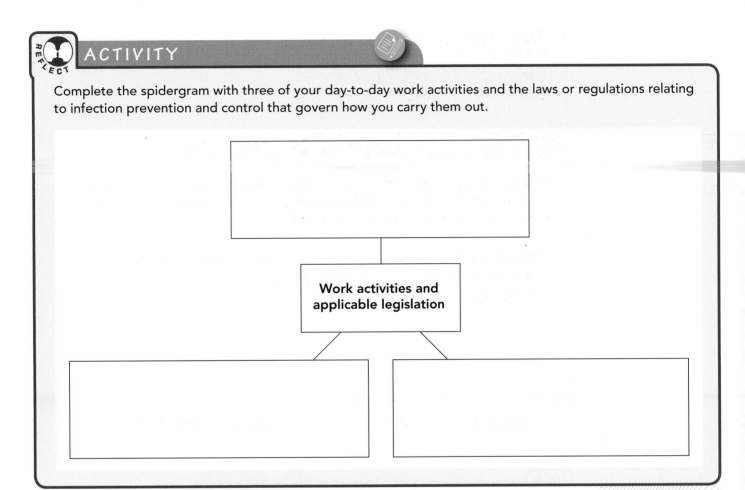

**Work activities and applicable legislation**

## ACTIVITY

All health and social care service providers are legally responsible for making sure they meet the safety standards set by **regulatory bodies**. Regulatory bodies include the Care Quality Commission (CQC), Social Care Councils, the General Medical Council (GMC) and the Nursing and Midwifery Council (NMC).

Use an internet search engine to find out about the infection prevention and control standards for three different regulatory bodies. Make a brief note below of what you find.

You could try searching the web pages of the regulatory body using, for example, the terms 'standards of quality and safety' or 'codes of practice'. Also look at the National Institute for Health and Clinical Excellence (NICE) website: www.nice.org.uk.

## Local and organisational policies relevant to infection prevention and control

Local authorities and organisations, such as the one you work for, publish guidance documents and policies that ensure the law meets the needs of local people.

**ACTIVITY**

Search the internet for local policies that will shape your work in helping prevent and control infection. Talk to your manager about your own role in helping to prevent and control infection in your organisation. Describe one of each below.

✿ Local policy:

✿ Organisational policy:

**Assessor tip**

Read through your organisational policies and procedures and ask your manager about anything you are unsure of. This will be good preparation for being observed in your workplace by your assessor, as well as ensuring your practice and knowledge are up-to-date.

# Systems and procedures relating to infection prevention and control

## Procedures and systems relevant to infection prevention and control

All health and social care settings have systems and standard procedures that aim to prevent and control the spread of infection. They tell workers exactly how to carry out their activities; failure to follow them puts everyone's health and safety at risk.

### ACTIVITY

Think again about the three day-to-day work activities you listed in the activity on page 215. Look at the procedures or systems you have to follow for each activity and make a note below of what they require you to do to help prevent and control infection.

✿ Procedure 1:




✿ Procedure 2:




✿ Procedure 3:

### Assessor tip

Reminding your assessor to observe standard procedures, for example using hand gel or hand washing when visiting your workplace, will demonstrate your understanding of the risk of infection and your competence in minimising this in practice.

# The potential impact of an outbreak of infection

## ACTIVITY

The Retreat provides residential accommodation with health care for older people and people with physical disabilities. It has just been hit by an outbreak of the highly infectious norovirus, also known as winter vomiting disease. Norovirus infection is common but very difficult to eliminate. However, following procedures described in an outbreak plan can prevent and control its spread.

Complete the following table to show you understand the impact of an outbreak of infection, such as norovirus, on residents, staff and an organisation such as The Retreat. The first one has been done for you.

| Outbreak plan procedures | Impact on residents, staff and the organisation | Reason for the impact |
|---|---|---|
| Make relevant people and authorities aware of the outbreak. | People associated with the care setting could become anxious, including family and friends. Bad publicity for the care setting. It could lose clients. | People don't know enough about the situation; they don't know how it will progress. The public will think the care setting doesn't practise safe procedures. |
| Restrict visiting. | | |
| Nurse the infected residents in isolation. | | |
| Isolate residents who are very likely to catch infections. | | |
| Employ additional staff to cover for sick staff. | | |

| Outbreak plan procedures | Impact on residents, staff and the organisation | Reason for the impact |
|---|---|---|
| Clean and decontaminate the environment. | | |

# The importance of risk assessment in relation to infection prevention and control

## What is 'risk'?

 ACTIVITY

1. Use a dictionary or an internet search engine to look up the word 'risk'. In your own words, write its definition below.

2. How high – or low – is the possibility of the following people being at risk from infection? Rate the possibility on a scale of 1 = low, 2 = medium, 3 = high.

   ✿ A young adult with moderate learning difficulties who is managing her own personal care.

   ✿ A middle-aged diabetic man with poor circulation and leg ulcers.

   ✿ A frail, older person with dementia, living alone at home.

   ✿ A person in hospital following keyhole surgery to remove their gall bladder.

   ✿ You.

3. What makes some people more vulnerable to infection than others?

## The risk of infection in your workplace

The previous activity showed you that the more vulnerable someone is, the greater the possibility of them suffering harm. To protect the people you care for and support from infection, you need to be aware of the risks.

 **ACTIVITY**

The wordsearch contains a number of factors – or hazards – in health or social care settings that can put people at risk of catching an infection. See how many you can find.

```
F  T  D  U  U  P  C  J  Q  V  N  H  A  I  R  N  S  N
A  J  B  R  S  M  E  M  P  I  O  V  Z  X  S  F  E  Z
E  O  L  I  E  T  J  S  X  R  E  W  W  G  E  T  I  T
C  T  O  N  D  S  W  D  T  U  G  J  N  I  C  I  R  T
E  P  O  E  T  I  O  O  I  S  P  I  H  A  G  I  S  A
S  A  D  Q  O  P  Y  I  P  E  S  C  T  N  D  U  I  S
N  R  V  R  W  X  C  J  L  S  R  N  U  S  D  R  S  P
Y  A  H  I  E  N  F  K  E  E  O  F  W  Y  E  P  P  E
D  S  R  B  L  U  O  R  K  C  D  W  T  T  F  P  U  R
K  I  M  D  S  F  D  D  L  G  R  L  C  D  O  E  T  M
I  T  M  H  T  D  N  A  N  N  F  A  I  L  O  T  U  K
S  E  E  Q  E  A  C  I  H  O  B  Z  V  N  D  S  M  U
J  S  A  L  H  I  H  F  E  J  S  E  N  S  E  R  G  M
Z  T  I  N  S  T  R  U  M  E  N  T  S  H  X  N  U  O
W  O  I  Y  O  O  Y  A  U  S  E  D  S  H  A  R  P  S
S  T  H  L  S  P  L  T  U  U  S  T  S  K  I  N  M  Y
V  P  C  M  U  C  O  U  S  M  E  M  B  R  A  N  E  S
P  E  Q  U  I  P  M  E  N  T  V  D  R  I  N  K  L  G
```

bacteria   viruses   fungi   parasites   pests   pets   equipment   instruments
used sharps   soiled dressings   soiled linen   used towels   food   drink
physical contact   mucous membranes   blood   urine   faeces   sputum
sperm   handkerchiefs   clothing   hair   skin   dirt   dust

General signs and symptoms of infection will be different, depending on whether the infection affects a local area (such as the area around a cut) or the whole body (such as flu). Localised signs and symptoms of infection include inflammation, redness, heat, pain, swelling and pus. If the infection affects the whole body then this is experienced as a raised temperature, aching joints, enlarged lymph glands, and a loss of appetite and energy.

## Carrying out a risk assessment

All employers must carry out a risk assessment in relation to the prevention and control of infection. You have a responsibility to be on the alert for hazards and to manage risks as you carry out your work. There are five steps to risk assessment.

1. Identify the infection hazard or risk.

2. Identify who is at risk, and how.

3. Assess the risk – can it be minimised or removed?

4. Record and share your findings and any actions that need to be taken.

5. Regularly review risk and strategies in place to minimise and manage the risk.

 ACTIVITY

1. Complete the following risk assessment for three hazards in your workplace that carry a risk of infection. An example has been done for you.

| What are the hazards? | Who might be at risk, and how? | What action is already being taken? | What else needs to be done, by whom and by when? | Done? |
|---|---|---|---|---|
| Spread of infection by people touching each other with unclean hands. | All patients are at risk, because they're ill and vulnerable. Unclean hands can spread bacterial infections such as MRSA and *C. difficile*. | We've got alcohol rub dispensers at the entrance to the ward with a sign asking visitors to wash their hands before they enter and as they leave. | A lot of people still don't use the dispensers. ✿ Ward manager to put up an information poster at the ward entrance on 1 September. ✿ All staff to give visitors a leaflet about the importance of hand hygiene and to leave a leaflet on bedside cabinets. Start on 1 September and continue. ✿ Ward manager to let all staff know about the poster and leaflets. | Yes. 1 September. Started 1 September and ongoing. Yes, at team meetings w/c 25 August. |

| What are the hazards? | Who might be at risk, and how? | What action is already being taken? | What else needs to be done, by whom and by when? | Done? |
|---|---|---|---|---|
| | | | | |
| | | | | |
| | | | | |

2. All risk assessments need to be reviewed. Why is this?

3. When would you review your suggestions for further action?

STOP
PLEASE WASH
YOUR HANDS

Preventing the spread of infection

# The importance of carrying out a risk assessment

## ACTIVITY

Complete the gaps in the following sentences using the words below. This will show that you understand the importance of carrying out a risk assessment.

adequate   desired   further   hazards   healthier
legal   reduce   risk   safer   who

✿ It is a _____ requirement for employers to carry out risk assessments.

✿ Risk assessments raise awareness of _____.

✿ They identify what the _____ is.

✿ They identify _____ may be at risk.

✿ They determine if existing action to prevent the risk is _____.

✿ They make you think about how you can _____ _____ the risk.

✿ They make you check that further action you take has the _____ effect.

✿ They help create a _____ and _____ workplace, protecting your health and that of your colleagues, the people you care for and support, and any visitors.

## ACTIVITY

Think about a risk assessment completed in your workplace regarding infection control.

1. What is the risk assessment?

2. Who carries it out?

3. How do the outcomes from each risk assessment influence your work?

### Assessor tip

Records of any risk assessments you have completed will be good evidence, so show these to your assessor. You can use them to explain why and how you carried out the risk assessment and what the outcome was.

223

# The importance of PPE in infection prevention and control

## Different types of PPE and the reasons for using it

PPE is designed to protect against **cross-infection** and the harmful effects of, for example, cleaning materials.

### ACTIVITY

Complete the gaps in the following sentences using the words below to show you know about the various types of PPE and the reasons for using them.

clothes   face mask   hand   body waste   fluids   single use   **mucous**
skin   hazardous   apron   disposing   goggles   gloves   food   contact

A _____ _____ will protect you from inhaling chemical fumes, **bacterial spores** and droplets coughed or sneezed into the atmosphere by someone with an infection.

Wearing a full body gown will protect your _____ and _____ from extensive splashing, for example by chemicals, body _____ and body waste.

Safety _____ protect your eyes from splashes of chemicals, body fluids and _____ _____.

Protect yourself when carrying out procedures that involve _____ with _____ **membranes** or breaks in the skin by wearing a _____ _____ apron.

You must always wear a disposable _____ when you're handling _____, cleaning, decontaminating equipment and _____ of waste.

When carrying out procedures that involve having _____ contact with any person, object or place that is suspected of being _____, you must wear single use _____.

# Putting on, taking off and disposing of PPE

## ACTIVITY

Use an internet search engine to find out how, and in what order, you should put on and remove an apron or gown, face mask, goggles and gloves. Describe your findings below.

Try searching for 'Putting on PPE', 'Taking PPE off' and 'Disposing of PPE'. There are lots of websites and video clips to help.

❁ Putting PPE on:

❁ Taking PPE off:

❁ Disposing of PPE:

Disposing of PPE

# Demonstrate the correct use of PPE

### ❓ ASK ACTIVITY

Ask your manager to observe you using PPE. You need to be able to demonstrate that you can:

- ✿ put it on correctly
- ✿ take it off correctly
- ✿ dispose of it correctly.

Act on their feedback to make sure you use it correctly. If you don't, you put yourself and the people you care for and support at risk.

Correct use of PPE

# Legislation relating to PPE

### 💡 THINK ACTIVITY

Complete the spidergram with examples of Acts and regulations that relate to PPE. The first one has been done for you.

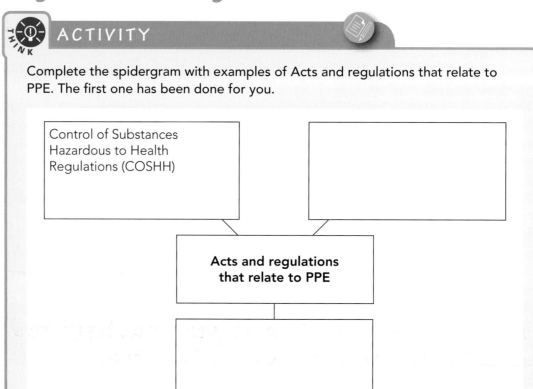

Control of Substances Hazardous to Health Regulations (COSHH)

**Acts and regulations that relate to PPE**

# Your, and your employer's, responsibilities regarding the use of PPE

### 💡 THINK ACTIVITY

Think of two of your day-to-day work activities that have the potential to spread infection. For each one, describe your, and your employer's, responsibilities regarding the use of PPE. An example has been done for you.

I have to help people use the toilet.

My responsibility is to wear the appropriate PPE; know how to put it on, take it off and dispose of it properly; report any problems with PPE, for example, if it is in short supply or poor condition.

My employer's responsibility is to make sure that PPE is provided and fit for purpose; train me in its use; write procedures that tell me when to wear it, how to use it, and so on.

✿

✿

# The importance of good personal hygiene in infection prevention and control

## Key principles of good personal hygiene

### Your questions answered...

There have been complaints from visitors that standards of personal hygiene at the residential care home where I work are not very good. I've been asked by my manager to give a training session to my colleagues. Can you suggest how I go about things so as not to cause embarrassment?

Personal hygiene can be a tricky subject to discuss. But it's worth discussing because poor standards of personal hygiene contribute to the spread of infection and make people rather unpleasant to be with. You don't need to make your training session personal – talk about personal hygiene in general terms because it affects everyone, as the complaints have shown.

Personal hygiene is about being clean, smelling fresh and looking presentable. So talk about:

✿ the areas of the body that need frequent bathing or showering, either because they're prone to harbour infectious microorganisms or because they're on show, for example the skin (especially the hands), hair (including facial hair), nails, teeth, dentures, armpits, and anal and genital areas

✿ the need to wear freshly laundered, neatly ironed clothes and clean shoes

✿ ways to stay smelling pleasant, including the use of deodorants and not smoking

✿ the need to follow your organisation's policy with regard to wearing jewellery and being 'bare beneath the elbows'

✿ the essential requirement to keep wounds covered.

  **ACTIVITY**

The wordsearch contains a number of requirements for maintaining good personal hygiene at work. See how many you can find.

```
B A R E B E L O W T H E E L B O W B
D I G Y Z N O J E W E L L E R Y S O
F N K H A I R T I E D B A C K W J Z
F R E S H B R E A T H Y G T G L C W
B A T H E D A I L Y L S Q N E R O C
C L E A N F E E T I L Q I D G C V O
S J M H T E A J A I C L R C S L E V
C D N G J B A D A G L N D L C E R E
L R D N Y W R N N E E R I E L A E R
E U C L S E D I M V A A Y A E N D E
A Y W A W E K S A E N E O N A N F D
N P H O M O H H B E C T D H N A E H
T B H M M S S Y S H L R R A H I E A
E S I S E N D L U M O I D N A L T I
E R O R A I A L D Z T P N D I S J R
T N F E T F E W C T H Z O S R J I O
H L L J O W U C O V E R W O U N D S
E C L N R S P R V V S Y J D K C Y D
```

clean hands    shower daily    bathe daily    clean hair
covered hair    hair tied back    fresh smelling    clean nails
trimmed nails    clean feet    covered feet    clean teeth    fresh breath
clean clothes    cover wounds    no jewellery    no smoking
clean shaven    tidy beard    bare below the elbow    no false nails

## Show you use a good hand washing technique

Keeping your hands clean is the single most effective way of preventing and controlling the spread of infection. You need to be able to demonstrate that you can use the correct technique.

### ACTIVITY

Use an internet search engine to remind yourself of the correct technique. Try searching for 'Hand washing technique'. There are numerous websites with easy-to-follow instructions.

## The correct sequence for hand washing

### ACTIVITY

Using the information you researched in the previous activity, create a poster that shows the correct sequence for hand washing that could be placed next to each of the hand basins in your workplace.

## When and why you should wash your hands

### ACTIVITY

Think about your normal working day and complete the table to show that you know when to wash your hands and why it is necessary. An example has been done for you.

| When I must wash my hands | Why I need to wash my hands |
| --- | --- |
| As soon as I arrive at my workplace and before I start work. | I may have brought an infection into work, for example from touching something that someone with an infection has touched. |
|  |  |
|  |  |
|  |  |
|  |  |

# Products used for hand washing

## ACTIVITY

Complete the gaps in the following sentences using the words below. This will show that you know what type of hand washing products you should use for different situations.

body   dirty   drying   fluids   no   paper   soap   towels   visibly   water

I should use soap and water or an antiseptic hand wash when:

✿   my hands are visibly _____ or contaminated with _____ _____

✿   there are hand _____ facilities, such as _____ _____.

Soap comes in the form of bars, leaves and as a liquid in a dispenser.

I should use alcohol solutions when:

✿   my hands are _____ clean

✿   there is no _____ and _____ available

✿   there are _____ hand drying facilities (because alcohol evaporates).

Alcohol solutions come in the form of rubs, liquids, gels and foams, from wall dispensers and personal dispensers.

# Procedures that relate to skincare

## ACTIVITY

Carry out a survey at your workplace to find out:
✿   whether staff know the correct procedures for looking after their skin
✿   what skincare products are available for staff to use, for example barrier creams, hand creams and hand lotions
✿   whether the products that are available meet everyone's needs, for example whether they are suitable for someone who has dermatitis or eczema.

If your findings show that people aren't caring for their skin properly or that skincare needs are not adequately provided for, talk to your manager.

## Assessor tip

Always remember to maintain good personal hygiene, not only to protect the individuals you care for and support, but to keep yourself healthy as well. You will be showing your competence in this area each time you meet with your assessor.

## ARE YOU READY FOR ASSESSMENT?

☑ **Do you know the following:**

☐ 1. Employees' and employers' main duties and responsibilities for the prevention and control of infection, including the use of personal protective equipment (PPE)?

☐ 2. The legislation, regulatory body standards, local policies and procedures for the prevention and control of infection and PPE?

☐ 3. The potential impact of an outbreak of infection on individuals and your organisation?

☐ 4. The definition of risk?

☐ 5. The potential risks of infection in your workplace?

☐ 6. The risk assessment process and reasons for undertaking this?

☐ 7. The different types, correct use, application, removal and disposal of PPE?

☐ 8. The reasons for using PPE?

☐ 9. The principles and procedures to maintain good personal hygiene and skincare?

☐ 10. The correct sequence for good hand washing technique?

☐ 11. The reasons for hand washing?

☐ 12. When hand washing should be carried out?

☐ 13. The range of products that should be used for hand washing?

☐ 14. The correct procedures related to skin care?

# Glossary

**ACAS:** the Advisory, Conciliation and Arbitration Service. www.acas.org.uk.

**Accessible:** easy to find, understand and use.

**Advocate:** someone who speaks on another person's behalf.

**Agency:** an organisation that provides a particular service.

**Agreed ways of working:** these tell you how you must carry out your work activities.

**Allege:** to declare or assert.

**Appraisal:** a planned meeting between a worker and their supervisor during which the worker's performance and learning and development needs are discussed, and their personal development plan is drawn up.

**Atherosclerosis:** also known as hardening of the arteries, this is a condition caused by a build-up of fatty plaque on the inside walls of the arteries.

**Attitude:** a way of thinking about something.

**Bacterial spores:** the structures that bacteria become in order to survive hostile environments.

**Belief:** something you think is real or true.

**Best practice:** in health and social care, this is safe, high quality care that responds to individual wishes, needs and preferences.

**Breach:** when confidentiality is broken or violated.

**Capacity:** having the mental ability to fully understand what you're told, make a decision based on that understanding, remember the decision and tell it to someone else.

**Care plans or support plans:** documents that describe the day-to-day requirements and preferences for care and support.

**Carers:** people who provide unpaid help and support to, for example, relatives, friends and neighbours.

**Communication and technological aids:** these aids include symbols, pictures, photographs, writing, sign language, interpreters, translators and special computer programs.

**Community life:** this includes health and social care services, education, employment, leisure facilities and private services such as shops and banks.

**Competent:** capable, skilled.

**Complainant:** someone who makes a complaint.

**Comply:** to conform, obey or submit to something.

**Confabulation:** an unconscious filling in of gaps in the memory that the person believes to be true.

**Cross-infection:** the spread of infection from one person, object or place to another, or from one part of the body to another.

**Cultural background:** the customs, behaviours, beliefs and values that you were brought up with.

**Data Protection Act 1998:** this Act protects our right to keep our personal and sensitive information (known as data) confidential.

**Dilemma:** a tricky situation.

**Disablism:** discrimination based on someone's lack of physical or intellectual ability.

**Disciplinary or misconduct procedures:** actions that are taken against someone to punish them for their behaviour.

**Discreetly:** carefully, cautiously.

**Disorientated:** to be confused, to lose your sense of direction.

**Diversity:** differences between individuals, for example, culture, race, gender, religion, age, abilities and disabilities, sexual orientation and social class.

**Duties and responsibilities:** work activities a person is required to do according to their job specification.

**Early onset dementia:** the term used for cases of dementia diagnosed before the age of 65.

**Equality:** dignity, respect and rights for all individuals, whatever their differences.

**Equal opportunities:** making sure that everybody, regardless of their differences, has an opportunity to access resources, such as money and housing, and life opportunities, such as education and employment.

**Ethnic or cultural background:** the behaviours, expectations, language, values and beliefs of the society, group and family in which a person is brought up.

**Faculty:** capability, such as mental capability.

**Flammable:** inflammable, burnable.

**Health and safety legislation:** the laws and regulations that are in place to protect us all from harm.

**Health Protection Units:** these deal with local public health issues. They are part of the Health Protection Agency.

**Holistic care package:** a combination of services put together to meet all of a person's needs.

**Holistically:** to care for and support the whole person, not just, for example, their physical needs.

**Incidence:** the number of cases.

**Informed consent:** agreeing to an activity or procedure being carried out based on the knowledge and understanding of that activity or procedure.

**Insight:** the ability to see into a situation.

**Interpreter:** someone who explains the meaning of words.

**Interventions:** in health and social care this relates to any treatment, service or activity that is used to promote an individual's well-being to prevent their deterioration or to support their current situation.

**Job role:** the function that someone is employed to fulfil, for example care assistant, health care assistant, support worker.

**Learning objective:** a statement that describes what the learner will know, understand or be able to do as a result of taking part in a learning activity.

**Lewy bodies:** tiny spherical proteins that are deposited inside nerve cells.

**Microorganisms:** these include bacteria, fungi and viruses. They can only be seen through a microscope lens.

**Mucous membranes:** tissues that line parts of the body that lead to the outside and are exposed to air, for example the lining of your nose and mouth.

**Multi-agency working:** where a number of different agencies work together with a common goal.

**Multidisciplinary meeting:** this brings together people with different roles and specialities who have the same aims, for example to provide care and support.

**Neutral:** unbiased, not taking sides.

**Outcomes:** in health and social care these refer to the effects or end results of services on an individual's life. Outcomes in person-centred approaches are therefore individual, as they depend on the priorities, goals and aspirations of the person.

**Parliamentary and Health Service Ombudsman:** this provides a service to the public by undertaking independent investigations into complaints that government departments, a range of other public bodies in the UK, and the NHS in England have not acted properly or fairly or have provided a poor service.

**Partnership working:** where professionals from different departments or organisations come together to use their expertise to best help and support individuals.

**Passive:** inactive, dependent on others, unwilling to make decisions and choices.

**Perceive:** to be aware or conscious of something.

**Perpetrator:** someone who carries out abuse.

**Perseveration:** repetition of a particular word, phrase or gesture.

**Plaques:** proteins that build up around nerve cells.

**Potential:** possible, likely.

**Prevalence:** the frequency with which a disease or condition occurs in the population.

**Prion:** a microscopic protein particle that transmits infectious diseases.

**Procedure:** a document that tells a worker exactly how to do a specific work activity.

**Professional boundaries:** limits that tell you what you can and can't do in your job role.

**Professional registration:** this is a requirement for some job roles in health and social care. To become registered, you need to show that you are committed to professional standards and personal development.

**Reflecting:** thinking.

**Regulatory bodies:** independent organisations, usually set up by government, that make rules and set standards for a work sector and oversee the activities of organisations within it.

**Respiratory diseases:** diseases of the lungs and body tissues that help us breathe.

**Risk:** the possibility of suffering harm or being exposed to danger.

**Self-administer:** to be responsible for taking your own medication.

**Sensory impairment:** damage to, or weakness in, one of the senses for example seeing or hearing.

**Setting:** a place where people receive care and support, such as a hospital ward or their own home.

**Sizism:** discrimination based on someone's size, for example, because they are regarded as too fat, too thin or too heavy.

**Stressor:** anything that causes stress.

**Tangles:** proteins that build up inside nerve cells.

**Translator:** someone who converts one language into another.

**Vulnerable:** someone who has a higher risk of being harmed, for example, through catching an infection or being abused.

**Vocabulary:** the words we use.

**Whistle-blower:** someone who tells the public or someone in authority about alleged or illegal activities taking place in their workplace.

**Work practice:** the way you do your work.

**Work setting:** a place where people with specific health and social care needs are cared for and supported, for example a hospital, a residential care home and the person's own home.